Full Circle

"A Memoir and WW2 Survival"

RENATA REBER

authorHOUSE®

AuthorHouse™
1663 Liberty Drive
Bloomington, IN 47403
www.authorhouse.com
Phone: 833-262-8899

Published by AuthorHouse 01/26/2023

ISBN: 978-1-6655-7910-0 (sc)
ISBN: 978-1-6655-7911-7 (hc)
ISBN: 978-1-6655-7912-4 (e)

Library of Congress Control Number: 2022923963

Contents

PART 2: MY NEW LIFE

PART 1

As I Remember - Through The Eyes Of A Child

RENATE RUPPRECHT REBER

Originally, I started to write my memoirs strictly for my family. Friends thought it was a rather interesting story and persuaded me to let others walk along with me down memory lane. Looking back, I had a good and interesting life. My memoirs are intended mainly for my family and future descendants to understand where they come from. Other readers may have similar recollections.

The script comes strictly from my recollection and memories, no specific research has been done. Dates and locations are true as I remember.

My Parents' Wedding 1934 – Therese (Resi)
and Theodor (Theo) Rupprecht

An Ordinary Life

An ordinary life! What is an ordinary life? I thought about it...... No life is ordinary! Every life has a purpose, every life is special. If we only knew what the purpose is. My life certainly was not ordinary. At least I don't think so. Even so I did not achieve awards or great riches, it was an interesting ride. I grew up in Germany during World War 2 which was an experience I don't wish on any one.

Children who grow up in the United States of America have no idea what a war is like, to live in it, to live with it and to grow up in it.

In America children go from infancy to Kindergarten, to grammar school, to High school, and maybe on to College. They play sports, date their classmate, go to dances, marry, have babies. Nothing wrong with that.

Then the circle starts all over again. Most people have siblings, stay connected with their classmates and have lifelong friends which bring them back to their school years. Some may never move out of their neighborhoods, their towns and/or States. Many never even travel to another country or have any interest what the rest of the world looks like or is all about. They live the "It's a Wonderful Life" type story.

I thought about this for a while and came to the conclusion (at age 81) that most of the above mentioned experiences don't fit my life.

As I am on the down side and in my early 80's, I am looking back to see if I can make any sense of it. I certainly don't have the ability to change any of it. It is what it is and was.

Is anybody going to miss me after I pass?

What will I be remembered for by my children, my grandchildren? Why am I here in this world?

I turned out to be a pretty good cook. Oma, can you make potato salad for us, the grand kids ask?

I do make a great German Potato Salad, and a fabulous whiskey sour, I might add. (not to be paired, please)!

No, there was more to my life and my family needs to know about it. There never seems to be enough time for my children to listen to my stories, to my life experiences and why this was not an ordinary life.

From left top down. Emmi, Marga, Rudi, Resi and Hans Schuller

I was born at the beginning of World War 2 and experienced the first five years of my life under the Fuehrer's regime. Adolf Hitler was his name. I am sure you all heard the name before. These first five years and the next five years that followed, shaped me into the person I have become.

There were good times and very loving times, however the atrocity of a war leaves lasting impressions. Survival is pounded into you and shapes you into the person you will become. I don't want to remember yesterday, but it is always there. Somewhere in the back of my head, these war memories are stuck and it took many years for them to emerge.

In my early years, only tomorrow mattered, only tomorrow counted. I was caught in a black tunnel for years and could not see the light. I was existing in that tunnel.

After I got married and had children, my life became a somewhat normal routine. I managed successfully to forget these early years. These memories were in my brain somewhere, but not quite ready to emerge.

It was better for me not to remember the years from 1943 to 1950, so I blocked it all out.

Little by little however, pictures started to appear in my head and I began seeing frames which had been blocked and hidden for a very long time and not to be remembered for many years.

How It All Started

I was born as Renate Margarete Rupprecht on May 13th, 1939, the only child of Therese Schuller and Theodor Rupprecht. My parents were married June 16th, 1934.

My Mother, Resi

Mothers name was Therese, Resi for short. She was born November 28, 1910. Theo, the short version for Theodor, was born June 11, 1907. They both grew up in the same neighborhood in a beautiful city called Wuerzburg, "im Frankenland", which is part of North Bavaria.

My Father Theo

My father was a mechanic, a good one I may say. He knew everything about cars and it's motor, (not many people had cars in those days). He also had a motorcycle with an attached side-car. Every vehicle my father ever owned was kept in perfect condition. He was a fanatic about cleanliness and he kept all his possessions in "like new" condition. He was proud of everything he owned (which was not much). In those days, you survived by your weekly paycheck. People were happy to have a job.

Many siblings were born into my father's family. A total of 11 children survived childhood diseases and grew up to become productive adults. They all lived thru WW1, so they learned hardship at an early age.

My grandfather built a fairly spacious home up on a hill, located just below the famous Festung Marienberg, the well-known fortress way up the hill with perfect views of the river Main.

I learned at a much later time (about 2020), the City of Wuerzburg had leased land to its citizens in the year of about 1900 to build a family home. These leases were written for the length of 100 years for a very minimum lease fee. That's how my grandfather acquired the land and he then was abled him to build a home for his growing family. The 100 year old house was just recently torn down (about 2018) and the land went back to the City of Wuerzburg. Now, finally I figured out why nobody in the family inherited the house, my one uncle was able to live there till his death.

The large Rupprecht family occupied this home, built on several acres of land and fenced in by an enormous eight foot high black wrought iron fence. There were two gates to enter/exit the property. These gates were locked most of the time and you had to have a key to get in. I remember having to climb up many stairs to reach the house. There also was a chicken coop with a chain link fence (within the wrought iron fence) to keep the chickens contained.

The family had a total of 11 living children.

Grandfather was called Opa. He was a Toepfer, (making ceramic cook ware, pots and pans). By the time I was born he had gotten involved in local politics. Oma was a small woman und always busy feeding all her many children.

WWI started in 1914.

My father was only seven years old. The years leading up to the war and during and after the war, were not plentiful, rather meager. There were many fruit trees on the land, they also grew vegetables and raised chickens. That's the image I got from the stories I heard from my parents. Still, my grandmother had a tough time feeding eleven little mouths three meals a day.

The family's religion was Protestant or Evangelisch, meaning they followed the religion of Martin Luther.

My Mother came from a family of seven children, two of whom died in infancy, five survived. They lived in Wuerzburg in the same neighborhood as my father did, somewhat closer to the river "Main". It was only a short walk to the Main and the beautiful "All Saints Bridge" or "Alte Main Bruecke" where we crossed the river just about every day.

My maternal grandparent's apartment, was located on the second floor above "Backerei Froehlich" a very popular bakery. The apartment was very spacious. Six rooms, plus a huge kitchen, large bath with tub and a separate toilet. I also remember several balconies, always adorned with beautiful flowers.

We entered the building on Zeller Strasse thru a large wooden entrance door with several doorbells located on the side wall. Every time you walked in, the smell of wonderful bread and baked goods welcomed you. This is an experience you will most likely never forget. Memories are connected to our sense of smell, which can be good or bad. In this situation it was wonderful.

Mutti's family was Katholisch, so I was raised to be a Catholic. It was customary that children were given their mother's religion. Wuerzburg and the region of Bayern (Bavaria) is predominantly Catholic. I believe there were only two protestant churches in the city while there were 52 catholic ones. The church my father belonged to was called "Deutschhaus Kirche". I went there only twice with my Father, both times on "Kar-Freitag", that's Good Friday. Vati held my hand during the service.

My mother's father was seriously injured in WW1 and paralyzed from the waist down being confined to a wheelchair for the rest of his life. He was a professional "Schneider Meister" (master tailor/dress maker) and was able to continue his craft and business sitting in his wheelchair with his two sons and two daughters working by his side. He died in 1938, one year before my birth. I never had the good fortune to meet him.

After World War 1 and the depression, my parents along with the rest of the country, struggled along and they made the best of their youthful years. They were married in 1934. My father expanded his talents working on motors, learning his craft as an auto mechanic. He always owned a motorcycle and at least one car and was able to repair anything and everything.

After my birth, my Mutti – the German word for Mommy - did not work outside the home. She was a full time mother and "Hausfrau". Vati, the name I called my father,w (the V is pronounced like F) earned enough (or not enough) money to pay for a government owned apartment. They payed cash for the furniture they purchased, except for a small radio, called Volksempfaenger.

This radio was very important. It was advised and recommended by Adolf Hitler, our Fuehrer, that all households should own a "Volksempfaenger" radio. (I believe it was made by Grundig) People were encouraged to listen to the radio, especially Hitler's speeches which were broadcast over the radio. Lots of propaganda! Any other purchases my parents made were paid for in cash. Money was saved (if any was left at the end of the week) in a Sparbuch in the "Sparkasse" the Deutsche bank.

Lots of music was played on the "Volksempfaenger", may it be Enrico Caruso singing an Aria or Opera, or military marching songs promoting Hitler's regime. My mother loved music, she sang along with every song and knew every word to every song. She also loved

Operas and Operettas. She always attended concerts and the theater. When she was pregnant with me she made sure I was exposed to the arts, especially lots of music.

Vati also enjoyed singing and dancing and having a good time. However, Opera was not his cup of tea, he preferred to entertain people with his singing and loved clowning around. By nature he was a happy man enjoying entertainment of all sorts.

Hitler also encouraged all sorts of sports activities. There were sports facilities my father joined and enjoyed, and we always had a set of "Keulen" around the house. (Big things made out of wood, to exercise arms and upper body). My mother exercised also and they both were members of the sports club, "Deutscher Sports Verein".

My parents lived a fairly simple but comfortable life and it appears thru pictures that they enjoyed themselves and had lots of fun. Father always was employed, they did have to watch their money but managed to have good times, good friends and fun.

I have seen pictures of my parents driving their little two-seater sports car, cabriole, with the rumble seat in the rear. They also enjoyed riding the motor cycle with the attached side car. I was told that they had several accidents, nothing serious, just many bruises. (That was before my birth)

My father became one of the original members of the automobile club called ADAC Club, (Allgemeiner Deutscher Automobil Club) and remained an active member till his deaths.

He was a big fan of motorcars, motorcycles and anything that was moved by an attached motor.

My mother Resi Rupprecht 1935

Picture of My father's Soccer team.

In the mid 1930's with Hitler on the rise, one of my father's best friends asked him to drive him to the port, it was either Hamburg or Bremen, to board a ship destination USA. People were becoming concerned and worried of the political situation. With a heavy heart my father said "Auf Wiedersehen" to his Jewish friend. As a parting gift and with much gratitude, his friend presented my father with two landscape oil paintings.

These two oils with their beautiful frames were cherished by my parents. It meant a lot to my father that he could be of help to his friend escaping Germany at the right time. The war was imminent and just around the corner. Unfortunately, the two friends lost contact with each other. I remember my father searching to get in touch with his friend after the war, but he was unsuccessful. He could not find any family members of his friend either.

The paintings are the work of a "Sigmund Wagner". My research shows the artist was born 1759 in Erlach, Switzerland. He died in Bern, Switzerland in 1835. These oil paintings supposedly are registered in a German Art Museum. I never was able to document that. I remember, after the war, going with my parents to a large Art Gallery/ Kunst Handlung with these paintings in tow. The experts told my father not to sell the paintings. "We will clean the art work for you, repair some damage and you will hang on to them", recommended the art dealer. "This is not the right time to sell." So my father took them home to display them in his living room. In 1996 I brought them to America and they are still hanging in my living room.

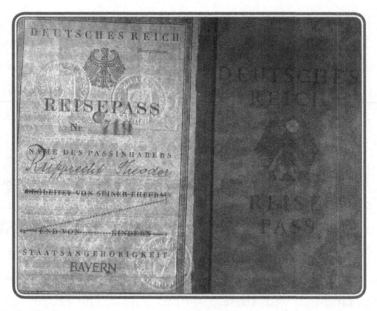

Father's first passport was issued in the year of 1926. It is passport # 719 of the "Deutsches Reich". My father was 19 years old.

The Paintings

Then Came The War

...and along came a baby.

1939! World War Two

Theo and Resi had been married for five years before I came along. It was a difficult pregnancy for my mother, with an even more difficult delivery. In labor for 28 hrs. I was delivered by a midwife with a doctor by her side. It was called a breach birth and it just about killed my mother. My father made a promise to her, "You never have to endure this procedure again" (delivering a baby). So, it was decided right then and there, that I was to be an only child. Mother had no breast milk for me. A neighbor who lived down the street supplied the necessary nourishment for me to survive. She dropped off a bottle every morning on our doorsteps.

I was told this story over and over again, how difficult it was to bring me into this world and keep me alive.

My Christening had to be shortly after my birth in the hospital Chapel, my mother being too ill to attend. Mutti had chosen the name "Beatrix" for me. My two aunts, (my mother's older sisters) did not like the name Beatrix, so they took it upon themselves and chose a different name for me without consulting my mother. (They most likely thought their sister was going to die). Aunt Marga was to be my godmother. She and Aunt Emmi decided my name should be Renate with Margarete as my middle name. This is how I became Renate Margarete.

My mother was upset about that decision, but she was too sick and it was too late to do anything about it. The birth certificate was signed and registered. Emmi and Marga were the two older sisters and domineering, they enjoyed telling my Mom what to do. After the naming rights episode my mother became obsessive with me. I was her child and don't anybody come near her child.

My two aunts were still very much involved in my upbringing. They adored me, mostly because I was a girl and they could dress me up and show me off. Being a girl was special. I had an older cousin Peter, he was Tante Marga's child. He was a beautiful boy with blond curly hair, but he refused to wear dresses and be dressed up. My only girl cousin Helga spent more time with her mother's family. She was the daughter of my mother's youngest brother and his wife Lola and at that time were more involved in her mother's side of the family.

At the age of three months I almost died. Whooping cough, bronchitis and rickets, all at the same time. I did pull through and became a fairly healthy child after I tackled all the usual childhood diseases, including chicken box, mumps and measles, the ones we have vaccinations for today. In my teenage years I had Scarlet fever, the flu and I almost died for a second time. With the flu and Scarlet fever, I remember the doctor coming to the house every day to administer a shot (injection). In those days, doctors made house calls to see their ill patients.

The first years of my life were happy years. I was spoiled by all. My father was drafted into the military/Wehrmacht in 1939, shortly after my birth. He was send to Frankreich (France) in 1941, where he spent all of his military duties and worked as a chauffeur/driver. Not all men knew how to operate a motor vehicle or repair them, so my Vati's expertise was in demand and appreciated. He was a very patient man with a good personality and he was very familiar with everything that had a motor and moved on wheels. He enjoyed repairing and fixing the vehicles and of course kept them spotless. Soon he was promoted to Feldwebel, Sargent in the Deutsche Wehrmacht, one of the armed forces of the Third Reich. He was in charge of a fleet of cars. In the following war years my father spent time in Paris, Le Havre, Cherbourg and lastly, for two years, in a prison camp in Saint Nazaire.

My parents loved me. I was their pride and joy and we had a wonderful time together. Mutti and I (that's what I called my mother – it is pronounced Mutte, with a short u (not you) a hard T and then an e), occupied a large apartment, provided by the government, since my father was employed by the Finanzamt (office), a branch of the government. The apartment was a walk-up situated on the 4th floor. My mother always preferred to live on the top floor so she could enjoy a great view over the roof tops. She enjoyed seeing the sun shine thru the windows and illuminate her daily polished floors. No elevator of course and we never did mind climbing the stairs. Nobody got fat, we walked off every extra gram. The stairs were white marble and extra wide. The railings were also wide and made out of marble stone and my mother loved to use them as a slide. I remember her laughing when she slid down at high speed. I was not allowed to do that – FOR ADULTS ONLY!

In his earlier years before the military, my father completed an apprenticeship to be a Master mechanic. His required schooling went to the age of 14, than he started his apprenticeship. I still have all his school papers and certificates, recommendations etc. in my possession. He kept every certificate, every school paper, including his report cards from "Volks Schule" and all apprentice certificates.

He always kept perfect records and logs of everything. He was proud of his penmanship and writing skills and it was very important for him to record his life on paper. Every day he wrote in a special log book how many kilometers he drove each day, what he did on a specific day, sometimes even the name of the restaurant where he stopped and what he ate.

After perfecting his trade as an auto mechanic working several years in very reputable workshops and garages, he was hired by the government, division of Internal Revenue or Finanzamt, as it was called in German, located in Wuerzburg. He loved his work as a master mechanic being in charge of a large garage with several automobiles. His skill of precision also enabled him to learn measuring and surveying. He measured farmland and acres of land in the country for tax purposes for Internal Revenue. He was proud of everything he did and was liked by all. Coming from a working class family with only the basic education till age 14, he took his job very seriously and always "enjoyed" working. There was not a lazy bone in his body. When someone was in need, my father was ready to help.

Mutti and I on the couch

Mutti did not work outside the home, she was a full time mother and had the title "Hausfrau". She enjoyed cooking and baking and keeping the apartment clean. Floors were washed and waxed and buffed on a daily schedule. Everything sparkled. I inherited that same gene for cleanliness, I like to see my house this way. She was a great mother, totally dedicated to her only child. We went shopping in the morning to buy the groceries for only that particular day. After all, we did not have refrigeration. In the morning, we bought one 8th of a pound of butter, Mutti asked for a half of a quarter of a pound, (I think it's the same, just sounded better). She stored the butter on the window sill of a west facing window in the morning, in the afternoon she carried it to the window facing north/east side, so it would not melt so fast.

Since we lived in the city district, Ludwig Strasse 25, we could walk to most any place. Up to the "Residence", we passed beautiful monuments, then down to Dom Strasse and thru all the little "Gaessle" (narrow lanes) by many famous fountains and buildings. We also had street cars available for transportation, so it was no problem getting around.

We spent the afternoons chasing ducks in the parks, Hofgarten and Klein-Nizza, then walked across the "Alte Main Bruecke" and the river to get to the other side of the city to visit my grandmother. On the way home we purchased two "Wienerli" (hotdogs) for our supper, (the butcher always handed me a small slice of the cold cut for tasting, a special treat), or my mother made her famous spinach with boiled potatoes. This was pretty much our daily routine.

My father spent all of his military time in France.

All food, gasoline and clothing was rationed in Germany beginning 1939. I had no worries, that was my mother's job. She worried enough for both of us, but made it all sound good for me.

Vati sent us care packages from France. These packages arrived regularly for several years as he spoiled us with lots of treats and gifts. Chocolates and Champagne, wine and clothes. I did not hurt for anything.

Vati sent Mutti and I each a beautiful bicycle, both red in color with lots of chrome. I could ride the bike by the time I was three and a half years old. Not much traffic in those days, I was allowed to ride on the street with my mother along by my side. We rode our bikes down to the river to go swimming. One day I got my tires caught in the trolley tracks, I fell off the bicycle and skinned and bruised my knees. The trolley car was right behind me but was able to stop just in time before it would have run me over. Mutti told me to be brave and get back on the bike, she will take care of my bloody knees later, or otherwise I will have to go to hospital. She told me to be brave like the soldiers who are fighting in the war. "We do not cry" was her swift answer. That was an order. So, I did not cry. "We do not cry" it was pounded into my head.

My mother's father was a master in his trade, a Schneider-Meister. Being well dressed and well put together was important to my grandfather and the rest of the family. His family always had to look good and presentable. He trained his children to always wear the proper attire. There were Sunday clothes, school clothes and play clothes, I kept changing my clothes. This tradition was passed on and down to the future generations, as I kept it up and so did my children. As soon as I arrived at home, clothes had to be changed and I put on my house shoes. Don't ever wear your shoes inside the house. If we left the house, I had to change into different clothes and shoes. This habit was carried forward. Changing clothes three to four times a day is not unusual. My clothes were always hung up on a hanger or chair, none ever landed or laid on the floor.

Grandfather's talents where appreciated by many. The tailoring business was carried on as a family business. The sewing room was huge with several seamstresses working for the family. My mother's family sort of were the early fashion designers for the middle to upper class population in the area.

My mother, being the youngest daughter in her family, did not get my grandmother's blessing to become a seamstress. Mutti would have loved to learn how to sew, sit with her older brothers and sisters in the large salon, (and pardon me, it was not a sweat shop), but she was not allowed too. I remember the salon with very large and beautifully gold framed mirrors where the ladies and gentlemen were fitted with their designer clothes. I was allowed to go inside the salon only at the end of the day to help pick up the dropped needles and pins with a large magnet. I tried to get as many pins on the magnet before they were put in a metal container. That was a fun job for me. My mother had a great talent for fashion also and she always regretted not being allowed to learn the trade.

My two aunts enjoyed dressing me fashionably and at an early age they took me along on shopping trips to the large fabric store to select and purchase fabric/material for the special clients. I was only two, maybe three years old and remember it well. We chose beautiful materials, silks, linen and satins for dresses for their well to do ladies and quality wools for the men's suits. I specially loved the silks and brocades and it was exiting when the sales ladies rolled out the huge rolls of beautiful materials in gorgeous different shades and colors. We bought ribbons and lace, needles and thread. Everything was purchased in the finest shops in the city, no wholesale outlets in those days. (I think the shop was called "Seisser" located on Augustiner Strasse).

However, making suits for men had soon changed to making military uniforms and the party dresses were not needed either. Only the most essential clothing items were in demand but people still needed clothes. Heavy winter coats were always in demand, dresses were also necessary. Men had to join the military and most women held up the home front or became useful with some sort of war effort help. However, clothes still had to be sewn at home, since ready-made clothes were not always available.

Both my parents grew up during WW1.

At age 14 my mother finished her basic schooling and it was recommended for her to enter "Handel Schule", two years of training for middle grade education focusing on office skills, including typing, short hand and accounting. It was a step above the rest. She loved shorthand and used it a lot as an adult. After graduation, employment was hard to come by. This was in the 20's and after WW1 the depression hit everybody hard. She finally did get a job as a retail clerk and hated every minute of it. I believe she was happy when my father came along to marry her and she could quit her job. Married ladies just kept their home clean and raised the children.

Both my parents grew up with Jewish children: they all went to school together. They lived in the same neighborhoods and formed close relationships. Later they went to dances together, but this was not encouraged. Christian girls where called "Schicksle", when they associated and hung out with Jewish boys and girls. My mother used the word "Schicksle" a lot, when she talked about her girl friends.

In the 1930's the Nazi ideology spread quickly to the largely unemployed population, folks still recuperating from the depression that followed WW1. Hitler promised everybody work and a good economy. Common folks and highly intelligent people started to follow one deranged person. The devil was unleashed and in command.

My father was home several times on military leave. During those days he taught me table manners, how to eat properly, something very important to him. I was not allowed to speak during meal time, the knife was held in my right hand and the fork in the left. You eat as quietly as you can, you always chew with your mouth closed. Soup was eaten with a spoon in your right hand and the left hand rested on the table.

There was a reason for the left hand visible on the table, I let you figure that one out. No smacking allowed. Every meal was a ceremony. My father ate very thoughtfully, maybe I should say with respect, like it could possibly be his last meal. Even a slice of bread with Wurst (cold cut), usually served on a wooden cutting board, had to be eaten with knife and fork. He ate nothing by just holding food in his hand, unless it was a piece of fruit. He always used a plate or a cutting board. When he sliced the large, dark loaf of German bread, he symbolized it first with three crosses on the back. The meaning was, the lord will always provide and we never run out of bread. Certain things my father was strict about and I learned it at a young age. I followed his rules, all was good and I loved him. My Vati was a good man.

I remember my Oma (my mother's mother) taking me on a trip to Muenchen (Munich). We traveled by train. I liked riding on the train, looking out the window, seeing all the fields (remember I lived in the city) and stopping at the many train stations between Wuerzburg and our destination. People got off and on the train, well dressed ladies and mostly soldiers. My Oma and I visited her sister, who owned a small hotel and coffee house in Munich. It was in the center of the city, very elegant and the name was "Café Fischbacher". There were wood framed walls with design, mostly small tables with white table cloths, the best china and silver coffee pots. I was very impressed with everything so shiny and highly polished.

I don't remember the guest room we stayed in, however I do remember in the morning we went down the stairs for breakfast to eat in the spacious and comfortable dining room. We were served by a waiter, a soft boiled egg and Broetchen (Rolls) and croissant, butter and marmalade. Coffee for my Oma and Kakau, hot Chocolate for me. My great aunt joined us for breakfast. Lots of talking between them, they had not seen each other in a while. I was not allowed to interrupt, but was expected to answer when asked a question. I had good manners, even at an early age.

I did not see any male family members; they must have been in the war. Oma and I went sightseeing during the day. We could not take up all of my great aunts time. Oma showed me the "Marien Platz", we went to the Viktualienmarkt and of course the "Hofbraeu House". She also wanted to see "Die Wiesn", that would be the grounds where the "Oktober Fest" takes place every year. We took the trolley to what seemed to be a long ride. It was not September or Oktoberfest time, so the area was not packed with visitors.

Our destination was the "Wiesn".

We found a Wirtschaft (Restaurant). My Oma ordered a bier for herself and a lemonade for me. She also ordered Frankfurter Wuerstle, served with mustard and a slice of dark bread for Oma and a Prezel for me. Our order arrived and the waiter put it in front of us and left. My Oma looked at me and then we waited. Finally she got the attention of the waiter. "You forgot to bring us table ware", Oma said. "Here we pick up the Wurst with our fingers", the waiter replied to my Oma quickly. "Well not where we come from", Oma said. "We eat civilized with knife and fork". He brought us knife and fork, not before he smirked at us. Now we could eat properly.

Another trip I took with my Grandmother. Again by train and we visited another sister of hers. She lived in Ponnholz, near Regensburg. Oma's sister Susi and her husband owned a small neighborhood grocery store on the outskirts of town in a coal mining area. I remember many tall pine trees in their back yard, chickens running around in a fenced in area. They had no children of their own but always owned a big German Shepard dog. The shop was in the front and their living quarters in the rear of the small structure. I remember a huge wooden barrel of pickles next to the counter and every customer just reached in the barrel with very long tongs and pulled out a pickle. When my great aunt was called to the store front by a loud bell, this gigantic German Shepard dog, guarded the premises and us. Oma and I were in the living room sitting in a chair when Aunt Susi was called to the store. We did not move for a long time till Aunt Susi returned. We were scared to death, frozen in time.

That's what we call a watch dog.

Wo Meine Wiege Stand

Where my cradle stood

My Family before the war

We lived in Wuerzburg, a beautiful baroque-style City with a thousand year old history. Wuerzburg was Christianized in 686 by Irish missionaries Kilian, Kolonat and Totnan. We had 52 catholic churches plus two protestant ones, obviously the region being mostly of a catholic population. The highlight of the city is the "Residence", one of Germany's finest baroque buildings. There were many more beautiful buildings and churches, famous structures like the well renowned university and Medical school. The Roentgen Institute with the first X-ray machine was invented in 1895 and was located down the street from where we lived.

The Prince Bishops of Wuerzburg first resided in the fortress up on one of the many hills, surrounding Wuerzburg, it is a huge fortress called Festung (fortress) Marienberg. However in 1719 the court/government was transferred to the center of the city. A modest castle was erected on the site of the present "Residenz Platz". Shortly after completion it was decided the structure was inadequate to house the many famous guests, mostly being royals and the residing Prince-Bishops. It was decided that a bigger residence is required. The court architect, Balthasar Neumann was selected to prepare plans and to design a new and extensive building without delay. The chosen city location turned out to be more convenient for the frequently visiting Bishops, Kings and royalties, of course also more impressive to reside in a much more spacious and luxurious "house". Magnificent gardens were added, which in later years became my playground, since we lived only one street away.

The Wuerzburger "Residenz" is one of the most important palaces in Germany of the baroque era and architecture. Today, Wuerzburg is also known for its many vineyards, wine cellars and wineries which surround this magnificent city.

During the war years, with my father gone most of the time, my mother did sublet a spare room to a student from northern Germany. The young man attended the University of Wuerzburg to become a physician. I was told he was a very serious student and he was good company for my mother. She liked having someone living with us in the apartment. I only remember him as very tall man. He spent most of his time at Wuerzburg's famous library or in his room.

The Early Years

As I mentioned before, I was born into the war.

About 1941 wartime became the normal life style. Our life revolved around the war. In the years that followed, we spent more evenings and many day time hours in our basement. Our designated shelter was the "Finanzamt" shelter, we lived in that building. Folks, who lived in the area were allowed to use this large shelter also. We got to know our neighbors and made friends. People worried about each other when they did not show up. Sirens sounded off to let us know the planes were on their way to drop their bombs. They were mostly British bombers. We ran to the basement for cover, as fast as possible. It did not take long to get used to the underground routine. Folks established small comfort corners in the large basement areas, which over time became stocked with mattresses, furniture, blankets and food. Some folks had a small radio, they spread the current location and route of the bomber planes quickly thru-out the shelters.

My mother also took the two oil paintings to our private basement. She buried them under a pile of coal. She was clever enough to wrap them in a sheet so the black coal and briquette dust would not damage them too badly.

Over the next few years, people hauled more and more furniture for safe keeping and comfort to the shelters. We had quite an odd collection of necessary items in the basement. An arm chair from the living room, one chair from the dining room, a mattress, blankets, pillows and candles. Of course some of the food, wine and champagne my father had sent also ended up in the shelter. When the air raid was over, the sirens sounded again, the coast was clear and we returned to our apartment which by that time was sparsely but comfortably furnished.

Our shelter was huge and under most of the building. Over the years, people constructed tunnels underground to connect the shelters. That saved thousands of lives during the last bombing attacks. When one exit of a shelter was blocked with fallen down stones, rubble and debris, the possibility was there to find another exit and they were able to escape certain death by suffocation. People from our neighborhood used the same shelter as we did, so hundreds of folks spent much time together.

The local folks were asking themselves, "Why would the "Englander" (Brits) want to bomb the city of Wuerzburg, since there was no significant military value?" We had beautiful historic buildings and churches. We did have a fairly large train station which was the north and south rail connection for the country. Another target of interest might have been the Kugellagerfabrik, a ball baring factory. Maybe that was the target they were after, or the enemy just kept sending us occasional warnings, maybe they were doing target practice bombing.

We also had several large hospitals in Wuerzburg and about 40 or more military dispensaries popped up in the area as injured soldiers were transferred to our city. All were identified with large red crosses painted on their roofs. The buildings were well identified and marked as care facilities. Apparently our enemies did not understand those rules as they certainly did not follow them.

June 1944, American soldiers liberated France. My father was stationed in France since 1939. I heard my mother mention the city of Cherbourg, the last known location of my father. I remember hearing names like Stalin, Roosevelt, Franco and Mussolini, Churchill and let's not forget Adolf Hitler, the creator of this horrible mess. Thru the eyes and ears of a child, I did not know what the adults were talking about and nobody explained anything to me. Our radio was turned on most of the time, as long as it was in operating condition and the electrical power was not shut off. I could feel the mood was changing and our daily life was getting much more serious. Maybe it was around 1943 when the care packages from my father stopped. The situation in our area became serious and dangerous by the end of 1944.

Before the major attack on Wuerzburg, March 16, 1945, our city endured 334 smaller bombing attacks by British and American Airforces, totaling approximately 400 casualties. They usually dropped several bombs in different areas and/or neighborhoods and gave everybody a good scare. The sirens went off with a blare and very slow and low flying grey/black monsters approached us. We said the "Flieger" (flyering bombers) are coming. It sounded like the buzzing of bees. The approach took only minutes, the actual attack took less time. They dropped their bombs, we covered our ears. Some people prayed, others held their breath. The damage was done. Somebody's house or building was hit, damaged or even totally destroyed.

I did not understand what was going on.

All this destruction. Why do we have to run to the basement shelter when the sirens went off, which is just about every night? It became routine. We did not wear pajamas any more, but slept in our clothes. Always ready and prepared for the unexpected, ready to run. The sirens went off, the sound of the bombers, I can still hear them, buzzing like a swarm of bees.

The sirens sounded again and we could leave the basement. Every day a few more buildings and houses of our city were destroyed. Sometimes people could not get out of the shelters. Doors were jammed, fallen down rocks and debris were blocking the exit doors. We crawled our way out of the shelter, back up the stairs to our apartment to assess the damage. Most the time we only had a few blown out windows. Our location was not what the enemy was after.

We did not live very far away from the Bahnhof (train station), which was always a target. This routine seemed like the norm of life at this point, back up the four flight of stairs to our apartment to pick up the shattered window panes and straighten out the crooked pictures, the dislocated and knocked over items including small furniture.

Why was this happening to us?

I did not know, nobody explained anything to me. People kill people, that is what we call "war". My mother did not explain anything and I wonder if she knew anything about the politics or the horrors behind it all. Did she have knowledge about the round-up of the Jewish people when they were put on the train? What was their destination? "They are going back to Israel, they are going home, to their land", was the answer. What was happening to my parent's childhood friends? Did she know about the concentration camps? These concentration camps were located quite a distance from Wuerzburg. However, I like to believe and will believe that she had no knowledge of the catastrophes of this war. The women only talked about their loved ones on the front line, which country their husbands, brothers and sons were fighting in, or how many ration stamps they had left for the week to feed their children. None of them could have done anything about it, they were totally helpless. Nobody spoke up or asked serious questions, "Obey the rules", stay behind the scene.

I never could understand any of this, but my eyes and ears were always open. I knew nothing but heard more than I should have at my young age. I was a child and everybody tried to keep me safe. Not that I would have understood anything if they told me. Three, four and five years old, this was my life, this was my norm. I was told "run schneller, schneller, (faster, faster)"! I ran as fast as my skinny little legs would take me, my mother holding on to my hand and pulling me along. Just try to get away from it all, stay alive. I did what my mother told me to do. We were only concerned about our survival. Mother mostly worried about protecting me, keeping a roof over our heads and where the next meal was coming from. I was o.k. as long as she was with me.

I experienced very noisy and destructive bombs falling on friends and relatives homes, the constant shelling, which I knew was bad. Every time a bomb was dropped the ground was shaking. Miraculously our beautiful apartment, my home, my mother's highly polished floors, my bed, my clothes, my toys, all was o.k. Oh, let's not forget about my dolls and the life sized, stuffed Fox Terrier dog with four small wheels. I called her Doxi and I pulled her along, all over the apartment. I was a busy little girl playing mostly by myself, since I had no siblings.

My parents never had to tell me that they loved me, I knew they did. It was not necessary or customary to hear those words all the time. I don't think Germans (by nature) are that very affectionate of a people, at least not in public. They are loving, but don't show it off with hugs and kisses in public. They schmooze in private. My mother and I cuddled a lot and she loved me with all her heart. She could not have taken better care of me or protected me more. It all showed in her loving actions and protection for me.

Hitler started WW2, the German people were under his control.

He motivated his people, promised and convinced all, that with hard work, good times will be coming along with lots of great opportunities. The regime will provide meaningful jobs for every Buerger (citizen) and let all people enjoy a comfortable existence and carefree future. Hitler ordered to build the Autobahn, even so there were not many cars to use it.

It did not take too long before Germany felt twisted and distorted, robbed of the promised future and a good life that disappeared quickly. The Germans had lost World War 1 and paid for it dearly. Now history repeated itself and the same people are paying for it again, for many more years to come. Of course I did not understand any of this either. The German people were scared of the out-of-control SS including their fearless leader, the one who promised them a good life. I did what I was told to do and so did everybody else. "Obey the rules", those were the rules! Hitler's underlying hatred for Jewish people soon took over the country.

Later on in my first years of school our history lessons stopped with the year of about 1900. We were not taught any German history from between the years of 1900 – 1945. This time period was not mentioned in the curriculum. This information was never printed and put on the school bookshelves. I suppose they thought if they don't teach us we won't find out, or they were too ashamed for all the horrible things the German NAZI's did. Are we not supposed to know the history of our country? We should not know what happened during these war years or learn from it?

We were ashamed to be of German descent and we did not talk about the horrific sins the NAZI's committed, how many people were killed. The country was devastated and destroyed. Later on I learned that six Million Jews were killed in concentration camps. How many German soldiers lost their lives? Europe was turned upside down for the next 20 years. Four million houses out of 16 Million were totally flattened and destroyed in Germany during this horrible crime called war.

I did not want to accept the truth, believe or acknowledge any of it. I was not interested in the past. Just let me escape, move forward and forget. Germany became a branded nation, full of shame of Hitler's atrocities.

Many, many years past, before I could think back to these horrible years, before I could face it, I blocked it all out. I only saw the future. I did not remember the war years till much later in my life. Now I understand what the words mean, "those who cannot remember the past are condemned to repeat it". So, at some point I had to remember and face the facts.

No flags were flown in Germany after World War 2 for many years and the National Anthem was not sung. I always loved to sing the National Anthem but was told to hush. Years later they decided to use the third stance of the original song only, the words were more acceptable and appropriate. I only remembered the original version. By that time I had left the country.

It was many years later on one of my many trips back to Germany when I watched a soccer game on TV. The German National Anthem was played and I was singing along, the original words, the words I knew. My 2nd cousin Valentin informed me I could not sing these words that the German National Anthem now has new words. He put the new lyrics in my iPhone so I could learn them. (Like I would do that) He was a proud German of the new Germany and the new generation. Enough time had passed. German flags are flying and the strong pride of being a German citizen has returned. But the motto remained, "Nie wieder" meaning "Never Again". Never again will Germany get involved in a war.

Living in a beautiful city, before the bombing, was wonderful. Peaceful! So much to see, so much history. You take it all for granted, which is normal for a young child. We walked across the Main River over the "Alte Main Bruecke" almost every day. My Oma lived across the river. Mutti and I watched the freighters float thru the locks or the fisherman sitting on shore with long poles catching little fish. Their catch was called "Mee Fischli" (small fish from the river Main), may be small smelts. They were than deep fried and people loved to eat them. I hated to eat anything that came out of the dirty water and to this day I refuse to eat any kind of sea food.

While stationed in France, the packages kept coming from my father, but less often, mostly chocolates and French wines. I developed my love for chocolate at an early age. Mutti always insisted chocolate was good for me, it was part of my diet. We did not eat much meat, also sugar was hard to come by. In Germany, sugar was produced from sugar beets, not from sugar cane. Once in a while we did get a bonbon, it was made from candied sugar. Our food consisted of what was home grown in our own gardens.

Mutti cooked potatoes and carrots and spinach almost daily, meat was a rarity and not often on our menu. Maybe an occasional chicken. I was a fussy eater, thankfully Mutti was a good cook. The vegetables from our garden were my main diet, besides chocolate of course. I also loved bread and baked goods, mostly made with yeast. Still my favorites to this day. Fantastic Kuchen, cheap to make with flour, eggs and milk and fruit from the gardens to arrange on top. I never heard of a banana, an orange or any fruit that was not grown locally.

My mother showed me all the beautiful churches and castles, the Glacee with its ponds and the river. We visited the many churches and castles, the parks and the residence with its glorious gardens, that was my playground. The beautiful "Neu Muenster Church" with its Baroque façade and double stairway was one of my favorites, I enjoyed running up one side, then down the other, than down to the catacomb as a daily exercise.

Down in the catacombs in the basement level three heads are laid out. They are Kilian, Kolonat and Totnan, the Irish missionaries who settled my city. They were beheaded, but later on awarded sainthood. Every year (I think it's in June for Pentecost) the catholic Bishop parades the three heads thru the city. Bavaria has a catholic majority of people and the religious calendar plays an influential role in folk's traditions and their lives.

Then we crossed over to Dom Strasse (street) and down again towards the river, what fun. On Sunday mornings a photographer usually stood his grounds or wandered around on Dom Strasse; he photographed children dressed in their Sunday best. We children enjoyed hiding behind the adults so the photographer could not see us to take our picture.

I had two cousins, Peter was three years older, Helga was two years older. All three of us went to Kindergarten, a nursery school for the young children and preschoolers. Helga's mother dropped Helga off at our apartment early in the mornings, Tante Lola had a job and went to work every day. Her husband, my Uncle Hans had health issues and spent most days at home. Mutti was concerned about me being an only child, so she made sure I had playmates and spend part of the day with other children.

I started going to Kindergarten at age three. Helga and I walked to Kindergarten together. We walked down on Ludwig Strasse, a very prominent street maybe a mile long. There were mature trees on both sides of the street and side sidewalks were extra wide. At the end of the street was the City Theater and just behind that was our

Kindergarten. Just the two of us, walking and skipping, I was three, Helga was five.

Can you imagine to send two little girls walking by themselves in today's climate?

Nobody worried. We walked together, she held my hand and we arrived safely and on time at the Kindergarten every day. We did not have to worry about vehicular traffic either, there was very little to none.

We had a great time, we played with our dolls, made necklaces, did crafts, group dancing and lots of singing. Helga and I became very close, she was like the sister I never had and I was her baby. She was in control of me and told me what to do and I did it. One of the Kindergarten teachers got married and I was selected to be her flower girl, probably because I was the smallest child. Helga was very jealous, she told me later that she wanted everything that I had. If we both had a little purse, mine was pink and hers was blue, she wanted the pink one. It was this way with everything. But we always got along well and became more like sisters than cousins.

Fresh air and exercising was always promoted and playing outside was the norm for the Kindergarten kids. On hot summer days we took "Field trips". We got to ride the trolley car to the outskirts of Wuerzburg. The city is located in a valley with hills of vineyards surrounding it. One day we walked up "Dallen Berg", all the way to the top. To the "Three Poplar Trees". My Uncle Julius owned a beautiful Villa up on Dallen Berg. My two older cousins remembered the location of his home.

After our snack called "Brotzeit" in German, the care takers/teachers told us to lay down in the meadow under the trees and take a nap. When the other kids and the teachers were asleep or otherwise occupied, Vetter (cousin) Peter and Cousin Helga woke me, took me by the hand and pulled me along and the three of us took off. We found Uncle Julius's house with the big gate and a tall wrought iron fence all around it. Peter climbed the fence, let himself in the garage and came back carrying a large ladder. He was 6 years old and took care of his two younger cousins. He lifted the ladder over the fence for us to climb. He and Helga were already over the fence, I was on the ladder, when a car drove up the very narrow road with Onkel (Uncle) Julius and Tante (Aunt) Lola. Tante Lola, Helga's mother, was working with her brother-in-law Julius, during the war years. Onkel Julius was well to do. He owned the best and most elegant cigar store in Wuerzburg, located on the most prominent street, Dom Strasse, that's where the Cathedral was located. Gentlemen came every day to buy cigars from Havana and fine Cigarettes. The store was decorated with a Koi pond, which was always beautifully maintained. The décor was very elegant and the shop had the best reputation, sort of a gathering place for gentlemen to meet for their daily nicotine consumption.

I was on the ladder when my aunt and uncle arrived. They got out of the car, took me off the ladder very carefully, placed me on the ground, than retrieved the two older ones. They got scolded and got Ohrfeigen, meaning slapped around the head. We all got loaded into the car and returned back to the city. In the meantime, the teachers were frantically looking for the escapees. When they could not find us they started their way back to the city. Police was informed about out our disappearance and helped with the search. I was only three going on four years old, so none of this was my fault. Everybody was hoping we would show up somewhere, and we did. The teachers started to watch us closer. From then on we were called the three run-aways.

The three of us had lots of good times together.

Since none of us had siblings, cousins were the next best thing. Peter played with us and our dolls, he always acted in the capacity as the father. He had a beautiful boy doll. I had a baby doll. We played in our small fruit/vegetable garden and we also enjoyed climbing trees.

Onkel Julius had four beautiful cherry trees in his garden and each of us pretended to own a tree. My cousins climbed high up in the cherry tree, while I always needed a boost. We communicated loudly with each other while sitting on a limb. We ate so many black cherries to get tummy aches. The red juice was dripping down our chins and we looked like we were dipped in blood. All such happy memories and good times to remember.

On one of his last visits home on his vacation, my Vati gave me a large Chocolate bar. It was divided into 12 smaller pieces. Maybe I was three to four years old. He said to me, Huepferle (that was one of his many nicknames for me), you have a choice. Eat one small piece of chocolate every day and it will last you for the whole week or even longer, or - you can choose to eat it all at once and it will all be gone the same day. I decided to eat one small piece every day and made it last for a very long time. I still remember that story and do it the same way today. One piece at a time, always have a reserve. We don't know if we can get more.

So, it happens every year, I eat Christmas chocolates around Easter time. I store it away, forget that I have it and sometimes things spoil and I have to toss it out. I just don't like to run out of anything or be without. I need to have a reserve, guess that comes from living thru a war. Everything had to last, like the food – another day, the clothes – another year.

Another thing my Father told me: When you have something new, treat it with respect. Keep it clean and don't mistreat it. This way it will always look like new, it will last for a very long time. So, I kept polishing my bicycle and it always looked like new. It was polished every day, whether I got to ride it or not. It was destroyed in the night of horror – I knew it was clean and polished.

These were good things to learn. So many of the phrases and lessons my parents taught me stuck with me and they have come in handy over the years. And of course "don't jump off the bridge even if all your friends do". "Be an individual!"

About 1943 life became more difficult. By then, electricity was rationed, so was food and everything else. Our windows had to be covered with black shades so our apartment could not be identified by the enemy. I was born into this war and I learned at a very early age that nothing was wasted, everything was saved, and nothing was thrown out. These early experiences thought me not to be wasteful with anything, turn off the lights and the water and eat everything on your plate. I was a picky eater but Mutti always cooked my favorites.

Most of the time my diet were boiled potatoes, creamed spinach or carrots. Always vegetables, I don't remember much meat, except for veal. "Eingemachtes Kalbfleisch" (some stew type dish made with veal and gravy with wine) was my mother's favorite, Mutti liked that and I shared only a few bites with her, since it was not one of my favorites. I think she used a little too much wine for my taste.

Cream of wheat was my favorite, made with water or milk if available, became a breakfast, lunch or dinner. However, I did not feel deprived, I did not know any better. This was the norm and I don't remember ever going hungry.

All the women were knitting socks and sweaters to send to the soldiers who were fighting on the eastern front, especially Poland and Russia. Even young girls and boys knew how to knit. Everybody at home was listened to the radio trying to follow and find out at which front their loved once were fighting on. That could be France, England or the most dreaded Russia. Winter in the Russian Tundra was descript as frozen hell and certain death. I found out later that I lost three uncles in Russia. They never returned home when the war was over.

The bombing raids became more frequent and increased daily. I did not know who dropped the bombs? Why do we have enemies? Other people don't like us? I am good, my mother is good. Our neighbors are good.

By January of 1945 we were pretty much out of everything. Electricity was rationed or not available, people ran out of coal and food. Schools were closed in our region, it was too cold and no coal was available. By this time, potatoes, our main source of food and the stored away preservatives of fruit and vegetables was in short supply.

The shelling attacks on our city became very frequent and happened anytime day or night. By now, many inhabitance of Wuerzburg had lost their homes in the attacks and moved to the country. Many folks had relatives living in the country and/or the many smaller villages surrounding the City. All in all, there were around 400 recorded airstrikes on Wuerzburg, before the major attack. We only had smaller direct hits during these years, just damage from the force of the bombs which were dropped in the neighborhood.

We spent most of our time in the shelters now and the living condition in the basements got worse every day. People ate what little food was available. Mice and other rodents were present. Cleanliness was not on the agenda any more, people did the best they could. No toilets, running water or power sources. Old people, sick people, women and children, everybody was afflicted with the usual winter diseases. Malnutrition was common and did not help the situation. No doctors or medicine available either, all went to the front to our fighting soldiers.

Rumors had it, "it won't be long before the end".

The attacking fighter planes showed up daily during daytime hours and at night. People run back and forth to the shelters, many just ran out of steam, they spend the time between shelling and rest in the shelter. Their main living quarters were now in the shelters. It was especially exhausting for the older generation, which by now were sick from decease, sick with worry from the daily stress.

Sometimes we saw the planes approaching us, flying low and they looked like huge ugly birds in the sky, all black or dark grey. They were humming and buzzing, very scary and frightening.

Schneller, schneller, run faster, faster, my mother kept telling me.

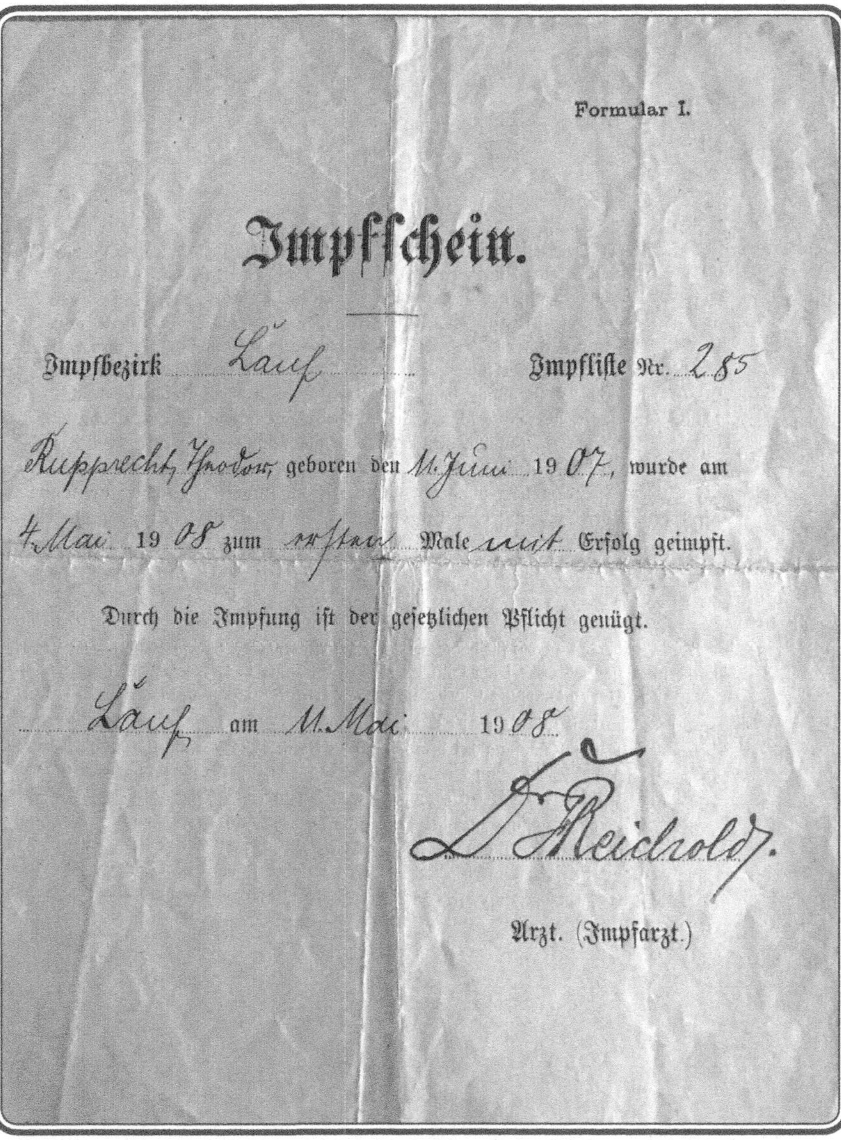
Formular I.

Impfschein.

Impfbezirk Lauf Impfliste Nr. 285

Rupprecht, Theodor, geboren den 11. Juni 1907, wurde am 4. Mai 1908 zum ersten Male mit Erfolg geimpft.

Durch die Impfung ist der gesetzlichen Pflicht genügt.

Lauf am 11. Mai 1908

Dr Reichold.

Arzt. (Impfarzt.)

Immunization

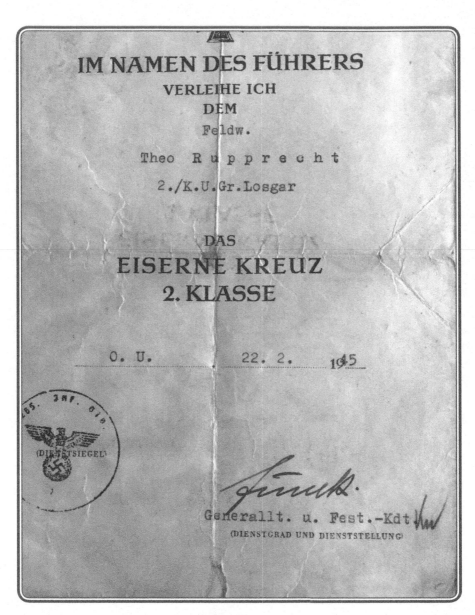

Iron Cross

Stadtrat Würzburg
Abt. Ehestandsdarlehen
Rathaus, Zimmer 80, I. Stock.

Feststellung der arischen Abstammung

bei

Ehestandsdarlehen

für

a) Familien- und Vorname _Schüller Therese_
(Bei Ehefrauen auch Geburtsname)

b) Stand und Beruf _Verkäuferin_

c) Geburtstag _28. 11. 1910_

d) Geburtsort _Würzburg_

e) Wohnort (auch Straße) _Kellerstr. 20. II_

f) Konfession (auch frühere Konfession) _Katholisch_

g) Staatsangehörigkeit _Bayern_
(Bei Ehefrauen auch die Staatsangehörigkeit vor ihrer Verheiratung)

Nach den Erläuterungen des Reichsfinanzministeriums vom 5. Juli 1933 und den Richtlinien für die meinden (Abschnitt II, 1b) vom 12. Juli 1933 zum Gesetz über die Förderung der Eheschließungen darf keiner beiden Brautleute bezw. Ehegatten nichtarischer Abstammung sein. Der Begriff der nichtarischen Abstammu bestimmt sich nach den Vorschriften des § 3 des Gesetzes zur Wiederherstellung des Berufsbeamtentums vom 7. 1933 (RGBl. S. 175) und der dazu erlassenen Durchführungsverordnung vom 11. April 1933 (RGBl. S.

Danach gelten als nichtarisch, wer von nichtarischen, insbesondere jüdischen Eltern oder Großeltern absta Großelternteil nichtarisch ist. Dies ist insbesondere dann anzunehmen,

My mother's proof of Arischen descent

The Night Of The Destruction

Friday, March 16th 1945 my world changed, all hell broke loose.

It was a beautiful spring day. Not a cloud in the sky. The warmest day of the year, almost summer like.

In the morning, our Student/tenant informed my mother he was taking a bicycle ride late afternoon, after his classes at the university, to pick up his wristwatch that was being repaired by my mother's uncle. This great-uncle of mine lived with his family in Hoechberg, a small village about six kilometers outside of Wuerzburg. Uncle Thiessen was, among other things, an expert of repairing clocks and watches. Our student, I think his name was Johannes - informed mother he was not comfortable spending the evening in Wuerzburg. He had a weird premonition. So my mother decided, she was not going to stay back either. In late afternoon they packed their bicycles. I was in the little child seat attached to my Mutti's bike.

My mother wore her fur coat since the evenings usually were still cold, being only the middle of March and we headed out of town. Mutti got off the bike and walked it up the hill. She took off her fur coat, she did get heated having to peddle with me in the seat and wearing her heavy coat. After all, it was such a lovely early spring day and the sun showed some warmth. Some gifts for the relatives were packed and stored on the back of the bicycle. It was an almost six mile ride thru the city to the other side, then up and down hills and we arrived about 6:30 p.m. The sun was going down and it was cooling off.

After greeting my great aunt Tante Franzie, Onkel Thiesen and their only daughter Doris, my mother's cousin, we went inside to enjoy a well prepared meal. Prepared by Tante Franzie, her hands were terribly disfigured by gout and arthritis. She was a very tiny person, bent over, and one of my Oma's three other sisters.

After the meal and some good conversation, one of the men stepped outside, probably to enjoy a cigar. That must have been about 9:00 pm.

He could hear in the distance a fleet of bombers approach.

The bombers were flying toward Wuerzburg. Their humming sounds could be heard in the far distance. We were summoned outdoors to listen to the noise of the approaching planes. Within minutes, the sky had turned green, than red (the Brit's sent planes ahead who served as target indicators who outlined the city). They were later identified and called Christmas trees. About 9:25 it all exploded. I got to experience and witness the biggest fireworks ever.

The humming noise was unbearable.

According to the records, approximately 224 to 280 two- motor Lancaster type British Air Force bombers of the #5 bombing group plus 11 Mosquito Hunters and American bombers left London at about 1700 hours and headed toward Wuerzburg and Nuernberg. It was an elite group of the British Airforce.

After the city was all illuminated by the so called "Christmas trees" they dropped some sort of phosphorous bombs and several other kind of bombs, targeting mostly the inner city and outskirts.

It took only about 20 minutes to erase this beautiful city.

No other fireworks in my lifetime ever compared or came close to what I saw that night and I have been hating fireworks ever since.

We watched and watched and stood in awe only to realize our beloved city was being destroyed.

Wuerzburg was on fire.

We stood helplessly watching the red skies. 20 minutes and this beautiful city was totally demolished. There were no significant military targets of interest in Wuerzburg. We learned later, that by March 16th the outcome of the war was already decided by the Allies. We learned the Brits had no specific targets in mind on that particular night when they flew in the direction of Wuerzburg and Nuernberg. Every city with more than 100,000 inhabitants needed to be bombed. Wuerzburg had 107,500 Buerger. A "blanket" bombing took care of it.

It was a tragedy to destroy this magnificent city.

Wuerzburg, which endured a massive bombing raid the night of March 16th 1945 had been the home to a little over 100,000 people. At that time there were also about 20,000 wounded soldiers occupying the approximately 40 make-shift hospitals, all marked with large red crosses on their roofs for easy identification, "DO NOT BOMB" Five thousand people lost their lives that night, 90% of all buildings and housing was destroyed.

Only about 6000 people occupied the city after the bombing, living in basement shelters or their garden sheds for most of the summer of 1945.

However, luck was with us that day.

We got out of the city just in time. We left about 5:00 p.m. to ride to Hoechberg. That was the same time the bombers left London. How did Johannes know? Premonition?

About 10:00 p.m. our medical student decided it was his duty to return to Wuerzburg and see how he could be of help. On his bicycle he attempted to ride back to the city but he could not get very far. There was nothing he could do, but turn around. The city was burning, Walls and Church towers were collapsing. No fire men, no help, just watch it all burn to the ground.

The city was 90% destroyed, 5000 dead in 20 minutes and more to follow that tragic night.

Of course we got to spend the night at the Thiesen's house. No place else to go.

About 1:00 a.m. that horrible night, my grandmother arrived walking from the burning city of Wuerzburg to the village of Hoechberg. It was only about a four mile walk, since she lived on the east side of the city on Zeller Strasse 43, the way to the village of Hoechberg. Oma, that's what I called my grandmother, smelled like ashes and smoke. Her clothes were singed and covered with soot and her hair was torched. She had taken cover in the huge bunker/shelter built into the hill, under the Festung, the fortress Marienberg. This was her designated bomb shelter. She was very familiar with the place and area since she had lived there all her adult life. She had been going to the shelter for the past years and knew it well.

Once people were able to open the heavy wooden doors to escape the bunker, they walked right into the flames and flying ashes, and it was impossible to get out. A young domestic housemaid who worked at the bakery in my Oma's building suggested they wet some blankets, put them over their heads and run for their lives. Oma told us later that night, they took the chance and ran over the burning phosphate sticks that the bomber planes had dropped along with other bombs. Everything was on fire and burning, but being at the edge of the city they had a chance, they made it out and kept running. Oma walked the four miles to Hoechberg, her sister's house. Hundreds of people who stayed in that particular bunker under the "Festung Marienberg" eventually died from suffocation of the heavy smoke.

I had to sleep with my Oma in the same bed that night. To this day I remember the smell of her burned clothes and leather shoes, her singed hair was the worst.

In the early morning hours, my mother decided to get on her bicycle and ride back to the city. There were no fire trucks, no able bodied men to help to put out the fires. Everything was still burning till there was nothing left, a city smoldering for days and weeks and totally in ruins. The wood of the many Tudor style buildings crackled away till there was nothing left. My mother did not make it close to the city or our apartment that day.

The next day she made another attempt to go back to the city, again no luck. It took her several attempts to be successful and make it all the way. She took along a small hand cart (four wheels and you pull it by hand or hook it to your bicycle as she did). She found some items in our basement, some homemade food in glass jars which were not broken, a silver ladle (my father had sent to her from France – I still use it). The looting had started and within a few days was in full forth. A large silver deep fry pot my Vati had sent from France, a specialty pot shaped like a large bell to fry Pommes frites (French fries) was nowhere to be found, already stolen. She told us, fires were still burning and only chimneys and exterior walls were standing. Fires were burning for six more weeks after the bombing.

My Easter present for that year was a beautiful big, white live Easter bunny with red eyes. It was placed in our garden in a brand new, large wooden crate especially made for the bunny, high off the ground, so no other critters could get to it. By the time my Mutti got to our yard, the bunny probably was somebodies dinner. She put the crate on her cart, she knew it would be useful for something. Later on it was painted white and was used in our kitchen as a kitchen cabinet. It served us well for the next five years.

My mother did not forget about the oil paintings, but she was not strong enough to dig them out of the rubble. She knew they were safe for a little while longer, they were buried under loads of rubble and the coals. She was able to identify the exact spot and hoped they were in a safe place. She loaded as much as she could in the cart, hooked it to the bicycle and peddled to Hoechberg. She made several trips. Johannes was also busy trying to help as a medic or where ever he could be useful.

It was not too long before Mutti found help to dig out the oil paintings and bring them to safety. She transported them on her small hand cart to Uncle Julius house, which was on the outskirts of the city up on the Dallenberg. The pictures were not badly damaged, mostly covered with soot.

When she returned from one of her early trips from the city, she described how the burned bodies were lined up in the streets for identification, all disfigured and burned to a third in size of a normal body. There were no streets or sidewalks left, people climbed over the fallen debris. For days, people pulled burned bodies from the still hot buildings/apartment houses and laid them out on what resembled sidewalks or streets, most of the bodies unidentifiable. Over 5000 city inhabitance lost their lives in one night. All were eventually buried in a mass grave.

Picture of Residence built in 1770

And The War Was Not Over!

The people of Wuerzburg tried to save what they could, which was not very much. They dug thru the rubble and maybe found some pictures or stored away papers from a safe, which had been blown apart. Broken furniture could be used as firewood, broken dishes might become a souvenir. Woman and children walked thru the rubble to make a pass trying to find their previous homes, all was destroyed. It was gruesome. People slept in garden sheds and burned out basements, in the nearby vineyards or woods. The biggest problem was food, water, and shelter.

This went on for months and most of the summer.

People who had left the city before the bombing started to come back to check on their property, their apartments. However it was not safe to walk around, the danger of structures collapsing was too great. Still, people kept wandering around aimlessly trying to find a place where they can spend a night.

Nobody had a destination, people were looking for family members, their neighbors and medical help. Within days the city took on a terrible smell of smoke, fire, burned and deceased bodies.

A huge hole was dug near the existing City cemetery, a mass grave was created.

Summer Of 1945

There was no counseling, no housing, no water, no stores, no heat, no food or transportation.

All thru Germany, people were on the move, running away from their enemy. Millions of people from all over Europe left their home land, may it be Hungary, Poland, Romania, Bulgaria, Ukraine or Czechoslovakia. Most went west, running to escape from the Russians, who promised torture, imprisonment and almost certain death.

They traveled by foot or wagon in hope to leave the Russians behind who were feared and known for their brutality. Most people were hoping to get to the part of Germany that later on will be occupied by the Americans, who were considered the better enemy. Some folks managed to get to America, others to England.

We called these people "Fluechtlinge", mostly woman, children and older folks. The Fluechtlinge were looking for the same as we were, shelter and food. They kept walking till they got caught by the next air raid or military on foot patrol.

Everybody was on their own and everybody was in the same situation. People from Wuerzburg were on the move, mostly on bicycle or by foot. They evacuated to the outskirts of the city or to the country side with the hope to find living quarters with relatives or maybe strangers who took them in. Everybody who had an extra room had to share. Our city was gone, our city was in total ruins. By comparison, after Dresden it was the worst bombed out city in Germany.

We were devastated and the war was not over yet. Lack of housing for most of the city's population, the lucky ones who survived, but who lost about everything, was just about non-existent. . People walked to the next closest village, maybe they found someone who took them in. The "Doerfer" (Villages) were in pretty good shape, they escaped most of the air raids.

The war was still going on at this time, but it was close to the end. The Volkssturm was called in to fight. All 16 year old boys and old men were handed some sort of defensive devise and ordered to put up a last fight for the Fatherland. The Russians were feared for being extremely cruel and nobody wanted to be their prisoner. We were so scared. All we heard "the Russians are coming, the Russians are coming". WW2 was on its last leg. It was catastrophic and Germany could not last much longer.

For several days after the bombing we could stay in Hoechberg with Uncle Thiesen, (our relatives) but the house was too small to accommodate us all.

My Oma stayed a few days, then walked about 10 miles or more to her daughter and son-in-law's house, my Tante Emmi and Uncle Julius house on Dallenberg. They had a one year old baby, cousin Spick, who was born in 1944. It was a beautiful home with large gardens and Oma's help was appreciated. It gave Oma a home for the next eight years.

Again, my mother and I had no place to live, we moved in with strangers but could only stay for a few nights. We were on the move. One morning Mutti took me with her to the city. We rode on her bike, me as usually in my little seat. (My beautiful smaller bike was never seen again). This was the first time I got to go home to Wuerzburg. I could not have found my way around but by mother did quite well maneuvering the bicycle thru and around the rubble. We stopped, this is it. This was our building. There was nothing left, a pile of rubble. When I say NOTHING, I mean NOTHING. Piles and piles of stones, no streets.

Mutti got a verbal message from a lady who lived in Waldbuettelbrunn. It was the next town over from Hoechberg. This small town is located about eight kilo meters south/west of Wuerzburg. She told Mutti about a room we could possibly occupy. My mother packed up the bicycle, I sat in the little seat attached to the handlebars and all our possessions were loaded on the bike. She peddled the bike for several kilometers. The bicycle was very shiny, all chrome and a deep red color, the one my father had sent her from France just a few years earlier.

We were spotted by a squad of fighter planes who immediately attacked and fired at us. The plane was flying so low, my mother told later she could see the pilots faces.

Mutti jumped off the bicycle, threw me in the ditch and herself on top of me. We were shot at, but missed. After a few minutes we crawled out of the ditch and ran to the very nearby woods, too scared to worry about our belongings. We sat for a while, shaking all over and I wiped some tears off Mutti's face.

After the fighter planes were out of sight, we dusted ourselves off and checked for bruises. Besides a small stone embedded in my leg, we were uninjured but very shook up. It took a while for Mutti to feel safe enough to come out of the forest. I did not mention my small injury and knew not to cry. The bicycle was bent out of shape and kaput, our last food supplies, the few glass jars filled with vegetables and fruit, were broken. We abandoned it all and continue our trip on foot through the woods. Now we had no food and the bike was trashed. We walked and walked, maybe in a circle. Mutti held my hand so tight, it hurt. We clang to each other and I knew she was shaking with fear, but we kept on moving. The sun was moving further west, not too long before it got dark and nightfall was imminent.

We had no destination, no place to go.

We did not know where to sleep that night. We just roamed around aimlessly in the forest. We came upon a narrow path and a marker pointed to the village of Waldbuettelbrunn. From the distance we recognized an old wooden cart pulled by a very old skinny ox, approaching us. The old man inquired about our destination. Mutti told him we don't know where we are but Waldbuettelbrunn is our destination. He told us not to go further, American troops were going to invade the town and take it over.

However, the old farmer offered us his empty house to spend the night. He just had vacated his little cottage-style house in fear of the American invasion. "There are some mattresses left and you can sleep there", he told us. The old man was sick and frightened and his wife could not get away fast enough. My mother took up his offer and we kept on walking towards the village in hopes to find the small and vacant cottage.

More and more cow-pulled carts and people carrying bundles of belongings came towards us, people were leaving their homes and town.

We walked right into the danger that the old farmers escaped from. We started running and hiding at the same time but unfortunately were moving in the wrong direction.

Mutti found the little old farmhouse just down the road and the shooting started from the other end of town. American Soldiers with heavy tanks were surrounding this small village and were ready to attack. The American invasion in this small village had begun. The remaining Villagers, mostly old people, women and children were prepared to defend their town and belongings. They put up a good fight. After two days of standing their grounds, the tanks rolled in and shot at everything in sight. The town was burning and we were in the middle of it. American tanks and vehicles were rolling in and shooting at everything that was in their way. An American Field artillery Battalion with heavy tanks stopped at nothing.

All black soldiers crawled out of the tanks and on foot, loaded with hand grenades to put up a last fight. In those days US military was segregated and this division was of all black soldiers. We had never seen a black man before and thought they came from Africa.

My mother grabbed me and we ran to the local school house for cover. Many women, children and old folks had gathered there. The locals were not ready to give up their town and to be defeated. American soldiers were shooting at every structure, they were aiming their tanks at the church tower which came tumbling down. They destroyed the school building and the little farmhouse, the one we never got to occupy. They parked their tanks at the edge of the town and continued on foot. We slept with all the remaining folks in what was left of the schoolhouse on mattresses for three nights, trying to stay away from the windows. Glass was shattering all over the place and my mother thru a blanket over my tiny body. The town's people had collected weapons and ammunition and managed to protect their town for three days before they finally gave up. After three days they realized they could not hold out any longer, after all they were fighting the American Army.

We left the school building and again, we had no place to go. We were still in Waldbuettelbrunn.

The local folks where running all over, gathering any Nazi-related artifacts, including uniforms and pictures of their husbands and sons. Nobody wanted to be associated or show any connection to the Nazis, to Hitler, or the Third Reich. Nobody wanted to be caught with mementos. They carried all these items to the back fields or garden areas and set them on fire. Everything needed to be destroyed. Fires everywhere, close by and in the distance.

Waldbuettlebrunn was captured and occupied by 2000 black soldiers. It was one of very few communities who defended their town and was fighting to the very end. The town folks were literally fighting in the narrow streets, American soldiers against old men and young untrained youth. They kept the fight up for a total of three days till the locals finally gave up. Mutti and I ended up at a private residence to take cover with several other women and children.

But not for long!

The American soldiers had stormed into the small town, occupied the village and made it their own. They broke down locked doors on houses to gain entry to find only women and their children. Some of the soldiers attacked the women, took advantage of the situation and ordered the woman to show them the 2nd and 3rd. floors. They pretended not to understand. We were so scared. The woman kept busy, they stood around the kitchen table and peeled potatoes. They did not take their eyes off the potatoes, we were shaking in our boots. The children were hiding under the table.

One of the soldier looked the women over and started to pick his prize.

He ordered his special selected one up the stairs to a bedroom. Rapes occurred along with other violent behavior. Just at the right time an officer entered the house and was told by the other women of the frightening situation. The women pleaded with the officer, trying to make him understand what just happened. He quickly went upstairs and fired his gun. This was a horrible and frightening experience.

At the right moment my mother grabbed my hand and we fled from the house, we fled the village and walked thru the forest, three miles back to Hoechberg. We stayed with the relatives again and shared one room with more strangers.

There was no more room at the inn.

The war ended for us on May 8th 1945 when Hitler committed suicide in Berlin. American soldiers crossed the Rhein River and moved east to liberate us. First was the "Befreiung" (liberation), then came the "Besetzung" (occupation). We were scared. American soldiers occupied the State of Bavaria, and other regions. Other regions of Germany were occupied by the French, Russians and English. Americans were our heroes, our liberators. The caravans with American solders rolled in, their trucks moving forward on the badly damaged roads.

It took American soldiers six days to take over the city of Wuerzburg and surrounding areas. We still had no housing and had to rely on the kindness of people taking us in for a night at a time.

My mother hooked up with the same lady from Waldbuettlebrunn, the one she had met a few weeks earlier. Her little girl was about the same age as I. She had heard of a place where we might be able to stay for a while. It was on an abandoned coal freighter on the Main River, just several miles north of Wuerzburg. The town was called Erlabrunn. We walked several miles, over the hills and thru the woods, the back roads to Erlabrunn. The owner of the freighter, a Dutch captain, had to abandon his boat. There was no way possible for him to take it back to Holland.

All the bridges over the river were destroyed, blown up either by bombs or explosives. Large stones and debris was floating in the Main River and all other waterways thru out Germany and the rest of Europa.

Donau, Rhein and Main where not passable and any kind of boat traffic was impossible. The captain/owner of the freighter started his journey back to Holland on foot. He allowed for us to live on his large transport freighter.

Our housing problem for the summer of 1945 was solved, but it was not all fun and games. We had a roof over our heads for several months, for the remainder of the summer season.

Picture of a Freighter similar to the one we lived on in 1945

Two woman and two little girls by themselves on this huge vessel. We were happy to find the living quarters clean and compact. There was a tiny kitchen and several little bedrooms with bunk beds. Nothing fancy, but it looked like fun at first. We ran around the ship, we slept in the narrow bunk beds and cooked what little food we had in the tiny kitchen. At night we were scared to death, the Gypsies were on the move from Hungary, walking mostly at night. They robbed, murdered and stole everything in sight. My mother and her lady friend could not pull the heavy oak plank (that's the very heavy board that connects from ship to shore) onto the ship, keeping strangers from coming on board. We had no protection. We listened for all the strange noises, sometimes a bird landing looking for food, maybe a mouse or a rat. We managed to "live" on the ship for almost four months thru the summer of 1945 and again, we survived.

My cousin Peter got to stay with us for a few weeks while his mother was searching for housing. It was helpful to have another person on board and we enjoyed his company. Another set of ears to listen for strange noises. He was already nine years old and I had just turned six in May. We explored the lower level of the boat. Some coal was still in the boat and we played with that. Sometimes my mother scraped together a bucket of coal to trade for some food with nearby farmers and/or village people. We washed up in the river. The water was deep, it was dangerous and we didn't know how to swim. We hung on to a rope.

That summer, I was in desperate need of shoes. Mutti and I walked for several miles to a man's house who hopefully could make a pair for me. I remember walking up a very steep hill. There was a small cottage in perfect repair and a lovely flower garden. This home was spared from the bombs, since it was located outside the city. The cobbler was able to help. He made a pair of sandals for me on the spot. A piece of leather for the sole cut to size, he punched some holes on the sides, a few leather strips to hold it all together and I was ready to go. My footwear for the rest of the summer was taken care off. The man gave my mother a few potatoes to take home, so it ended up being a successful day.

Tante Marga helped out with sewing some skirts and blouses all by hand (her sewing machine was destroyed). She used some left over materials, which she had salvaged from her basement. I had started to grow a bit. No hand-me-downs, nothing here to hand down. We had an extremely limited ward robe, more like no clothes and what I had did not fit. A skirt barely covered my bottom. Sometimes Tante Marga just lengthened a skirt adding more fabric from another piece of clothing, either at the bottom or the waist and I was good to go. Mutti had a bigger problem with her wardrobe.

She wore the same clothes every day till Tante Marga was able to find a sewing machine and more materials. They used military blankets to sew coats for the winter, flour sacks for dresses and pants for boys. It was great when somebody found a Parachute in the woods. Very desirable silk material, good for blouses, skirts and dresses.

I don't want to repeat myself but don't forget, we had nothing. Nothing means nothing. No help, no aid, no counseling, no food, except what we could find in the field. Also no communication system. People scratched a name and address on a stone or rock to inform their loved once of their where-about.

Cousin Peter and I played in the fields across from "our ship" and ate poppy seeds. We opened the capsules and dug out the fresh seeds. Yummy stuff. There were no stores/shops to purchase anything and we basically waited for our luck to run out.

There also was no government to organize anything. They had to get organized the same as we did. The American military helped the local government to get back on its feet; it took not long till the Americans gained control, we were "occupied".

Mutti was determined, she did not give up, she knew we had to survive. I don't know how my mother made soup out of nothing, we searched in the fields for lefts over vegetables and a few potatoes somebody ahead of us had dropped. "Wo ein Wille ist, ist ein Weg" meaning "Were there is a will, there is a way". That's what she said, she always had some clever words on hand.

Some of the farmers where kind enough to share, others were not. There were kind folks and many just the opposite, some resented us, the refugees from the city. The officials told the locals they had to share their homes and spare rooms, it was an order. Most farmers did not experience the devastation we did, the city people.

My mother, a petite woman 5'2", weight less than 90 lbs. She owned one pair of shoes. These shoes had a small heel. She wore the same pair of navy blue shoes for years. When the soles had worn out, she went to the cobbler and while she waited he made the necessary repairs. Sometimes the shoes needed new heels or only a tip. I have never seen a different pair of shoes on her. She did not complain. It was more important to find shoes for me, I was growing a bit. But she stayed strong, mostly for me.

To this day I have a difficult time trying to understand how my mother must have felt not being able to provide properly for her child or being able to answer the questions her child would ask. To certain things there just were no answers. Always holding my hand, we moved ahead, not knowing where to live, from one day to the next, with help and/or assistance from kind people. The constant question was, where do we find the next slice of bread or where do we lay our heads. She kept telling me, you must be strong, you cannot cry, we will survive. The government was of no help in these early weeks and months, there really was no government.

Germany was defeated and laid in ruins. The country's

transportation system did not exist, it was at a standstill. Water and sewer systems were destroyed, people were facing hunger and diseases and malnutrition was on the rise. No doctors were available for the people left behind. Everybody was at a standstill and ready for a nervous breakdown.

During that summer of 1945 my mother and I walked back to Wuerzburg along the river, trying to find and connect with old friends. We found a family, a mother and her disabled husband plus their three teenage daughters, friends of my Mutti's from happier times. They were living at the same address in their bombed-out residence without glass in the window frames and the roof half way blown off. They made several rooms livable at least for the summer months.

Some things were functional in their kitchen. There was an old stove to cook on, a sink and water was collected from a different sources. My mother accepted a cup of freshly brewed malt coffee. She said it was good but made a funny face. She told me later it did not resemble to any kind of coffee, the water was warm but not safe to consume. My eyes wandered. Above their kitchen stove, which was heated by wood and coal and used for cooking, was a make-shift clothes line. There were washed rags drying. I had no idea what these were used for but the ugly picture stuck in my mind. These rags were the only things their daughters had to use when they had their period. The rags were always in use, they were shared between the mother and the three girls. Washed and rinsed and used.

Down the hall lived a young mother with her infant. My Mutti knew her also from her earlier days. We stopped to say hello. She occupied a small room. The baby was in a carriage while she was searching for news flyers (pieces of paper that were dropped occasionally by planes to inform the leftover population regarding important news events and changes thru-out the country) to use as diapers. Not even plain paper was available. We visited with her also. Her husband was missing somewhere on the front. The stench was awful and we were glad to leave and make the long seven mile walk back to our freighter. At least we had fresh air on our boat, lots of it. We did appreciate that!

On the long way home, along the river, we were hungry. We found some fallen down fruit and helped ourselves. Most of the fruit was picked before it could ripen. We picked up the ones that had fallen to the ground and even the birds had rejected. Soon we passed by an old oak grove and picked the nuts of the ground.

An outbreak of typhoid and diphtheria hit the area. My grandmother contracted typhoid and had to be admitted to one of the heavily bombed-out hospitals in the city. There were a few undamaged rooms in use, and with a little bit of luck and connections (through Uncle Julius) she was admitted to a room on the 2nd floor. Visiting was not allowed. I remember my mother and I walking all the way from Erlabrunn thru the city of Wuerzburg to the other side of the city to Grombuehl where the Ludwig Spital/hospital was located. Tante Emmi joined us with a basket of beautiful red cherries harvested from her cherry trees.

We were not allowed to visit my Oma in her hospital room. We stood in the courtyard of the hospital, tossed a robe up to my grandmother's room for her to catch. We tied the rope to the basket and she pulled the basket up. Of course we did not know that fresh fruit was doing her more harm than good. She survived and was released after a few weeks stay. She "was terribly skinny when discharged from the hospital and we were not expecting for her to survive. Luckily she could move back in with Uncle Julius and Aunt

Emmi and their one year old son Spick. She loved taking care of the baby and he became her most cared for grandchild.

Summer was almost over. No way could we survive the winter on the barge. We had to move. Where too, was the big question?

I had turned six years old in May 1945; the war was officially over on May 8th 1945. I was supposed to start school in the fall. The German education system was at a standstill. No school buildings or teachers. Nuns, which we had plenty of, had to take over the education system. They also took care of the sick folks who were treated in the few remaining hospitals or, should I say what used to be hospitals. There were a lot of nuns around, they all spent the war years in the safety of their convent, praying and singing.

August 6th 1945 the Atom bomb was dropped on Hiroshima, Japan. We heard that on the small radio on our ship.

During the summer months of 1945, some clean-up had started in the city.

An American military officer, Let. John D. Skilton had the foresight to recognize the tremendous losses of all the beautiful buildings, famous churches and landmarks, caused by the bombings, especially the world famous "Residence". He ordered temporary repairs, which foremost included covering of the damaged roofs and ceilings of the main rooms of this well-known landmark. It took several months and lots of hard work by many American soldiers, who had recognized the need of immediate repair of this famous structure. Had they not done so, it would have been a tremendous loss to our city of Wuerzburg.

Lieutenant Skilton promptly obtained the necessary slates, tarps and wood for the temporary protection of the beautiful fresco ceilings of the residence and the "Hof Kirche". This art loving officer of the US Military recognized the importance to protect the magnificent antique paintings and remaining furnishings. Tarps from military trucks were used to cover the heavily damaged roofs to save the structures from more damage thru rain and snow which would certainly have caused total destruction of this world famous and magnificent old "Residence".

The Post War Years

My mother managed to find some living quarters for us in Hoechberg. Two tiny rooms on the 3rd floor under the roof of a nice one-family villa. Two families already shared and occupied the 2nd floor, Mutti and I ended up with the empty space in the attic. All home owners had to give up space and share their houses with refugees from the east and/or evacuees from the city. Most preferred to share with the folks from the city, if they had a choice, at least they spoke the same language. The owners occupied the ground level with their two teenage sons.

Part of the attic was finished off, divided into two small rooms, if you could call them rooms. Mutti separated the space with a curtain made from an American army blanket. She managed to get a bed for me which actually was a large crib. Imagine, I had to sleep in a crib. I think when Mutti told me of our good fortune that we found a place to live, I thought it would look like our apartment in the city. The first night I refused to lay down in the crib. It was the only bed someone could spare and my mother could find for me. She slept on the floor. I did not just cry, I screamed and cried my eyes out. I remember pounding with my hands on the frame of the crib till my hands hurt. I was six years old and too big for a crib. I think all of the bottled up anger let loose and I had a crying attack. I asked to be back in my own bed in the city. I cried and cried to no avail, I was stuck and slept in that crib for a long time. I think my mother and I both suffered from severe PTSD and the last stressful years had caught up with both of us.

No bathroom, no water on the 3rd. floor. A bucket with a flat board to sit on was our makeshift toilet. Mutti carried water upstairs collected from an outdoor faucet for our daily use, it also had to be carried back down two flights of stairs. The "toilet" bucket had to get carried down the stairs to be emptied outside to the "Mist Haufen", a manure pile in the back yard, which was used for animal and human waste.

The owners of the property had an acre of land and raised small farm animals to help with the food supply. They raised chickens, ducks, geese and a pig plus potatoes in a small garden. They were not the kindest or most generous kind of folks, did not care to share any of their food and I began to question the "kindness" of people. These folks resented us, since they were ordered to share their home. My Mutti became sickly for many years and was suffering greatly. The war years had caught up with her.

Occasionally the owners of the house took a chicken from the coop and put it on the tree stump. With a hatchet one of the boys chopped off the head of the chicken. That chicken kept on flying and walking around for a short while without a head. We kids piled on top of each other on a toilet seat, peeking thru a small window, to watch the torture, a scene from Grimm's "Bremer Stadt Musikanten". Some were cheering!

A pig was slaughtered once a year and a soup was cooked in the wash kettle, the same kettle which was used for boiling dirty laundry. Again, we kids climbed on the toilet and on top of each other to get a view thru the small window to see the pig being shot in the head and then fall to the ground. It was our entertainment.

They cooked "Kesselsuppe" meaning kettle soup. They put all the bones and skin plus the hoofs of the pig in the wash Kettle, made a fire underneath and boiled the water for hours turning it into what was later identified as a broth. Some sort of dumplings made of flour, pork fat and water was added at the end. All the families in the house got to pick up a tin pot full of broth. Of course we did not get to eat any of the meat. We were thankful to the neighbors for their kindness to share.

We had the same menu every day of the week. A pot of potatoes was boiled on Monday. This way we had to cook potatoes only one time of the week (save on coal) and they were readily available for the rest of the week to be used for potato salad, fried potatoes or any other potato creation. Mondays we ate Potato Soup, Tuesday Pea Soup, Wednesdays was Lentil Soup and so on. My mother was able to make soup from water and browned cream of wheat. Fried potatoes with onions, fried in a fry pan that was never washed, was one of my favorites. The grease in the pan had to be saved for the next dish.

People did become very creative and managed to cook with very little. Saturday, if lucky, my mother got a bone from the local butcher to cook as broth. That broth was used as a base for the many other dishes and or soups she cooked. On Sunday, maybe someone shared part of a rabbit which was killed in the nearby forest a few days earlier. Eggs were always a specialty when available. We walked five miles to Tante Emmi's house, hoping she could spare and give us two eggs.

We ate Pfannenkuchen (pancakes) made from flour, water and maybe an egg, some milk from the neighbor's goat, if he had enough to share. The pancakes were served with applesauce made from the apples which were stolen from some nearby trees. Mostly we picked the ones on the ground. Most foods were prepared with either potatoes or flour. We picked berries in the near-by forest, the same forest between Hoechberg und Waldbuettelbrunn, the one we had walked many times before.

The kids who lived in the house played together, Erika, maybe 2 years older than I and Klaus 8 years older. We went to pick berries, mushrooms and nuts. As long as it was not poisoned, we ate it. People shot rabbits and other small animals. I was a small and very skinny child, we had no milk to drink. A neighbor kept a goat. He was kind enough to give my mother a pint of goat milk, whenever he could spare it. Did you ever drink goat milk? The taste is terrible. So my mother made some kind of pudding which I managed to eat.

My Aunt Lola and Cousin Helga found housing on another hill above Wuerzburg, called "Neue Welt" just below the Frankenwarte. They occupied one large room which they divided by curtains into several smaller rooms. Uncle Hans, Helga's father came home from the war with injuries. They lived there for six years. During those years they had another baby, called Hans.

Tante Marga and Peter found housing in another small village, Onkel Emil came home when the war ended.

All of my extended family eventually found temporary housing, all spread six to 10 kilometers apart. Nobody thought the temporary housing would turn into five to ten years. No public transportation available, very few vehicles. It was a difficult time to visit each other. Very few had bicycles that had survived the war.

One of my mother's brothers, Rudi and three of my father's brothers, never returned home from the front.

My mother developed stomach ulcers and had to be hospitalized several times in the coming years. The war years had caught up with her. During the next five years she spend at least four weeks each year in hospital/sanitarium, sometimes even twice a year.

My father was still missing, we had not heard from him in more than three years.

There was no one available to take care of me during my mother's hospital stays. Nobody had space available or an extra bed. My Aunt Resi (same name as my mother's and a sister-in-law of my father) who was also bombed out from the city along with her only son, my cousin Erwin, also had found housing in Hoechberg. They took me in for one summer while Mutti was hospitalized for four weeks. Cousin Erwin and I became friends. Erwin was about 16 years old at that time and he had a speech impediment, he was a stutterer. However he could play the accordion very well and earned a little money playing music for local barn dances. His father was still missing in the war, we found out later, he was killed on the Russian front.

Erwin was also an only child, like me, as we all were. During the war years families did not produce children. The men were all in the war and it was considered irresponsible to put a child on this earth during war time. So, many couples were and remained childless. Of course all the men where gone off fighting in the war, got killed or imprisoned. It was a bad world and I lived right thru it. On my father's side were 11 siblings, only six of eleven produced one child each. The Ruppercht's side of the family got quite small.

Hearing Erwin play the accordion was wonderful, it became my dream and I wanted to learn how to play the instrument also. Several years later after finishing his studies in engineering, (which was constantly interrupted) Erwin immigrated to Switzerland were he still lives with his wife Hannelore. I got to see him for the first time in 2014 after 60 years at a small family reunion. He has a son and a daughter. His only son produced two sons of which one was killed in 2021 in a motorcycle accident.

Soon again, my mother had to be admitted to hospital. This time,

I could not stay with Tante Resi. My mother needed to hire someone to take care of me. She chose an 18 year old Farmer's daughter from the village who moved in with me. She cooked for me and curled my hair with a hot iron and got me ready for school. Her name was Olga and she was fun. Well, when my Mutti came home from the hospital, still recuperating and needing lots of help and rest, Olga became our maid. Remember, we had nothing and our so called apartment consisted of two tiny rooms. She was more of a companion to my mother and a Nanny to me. She cooked and kept our tiny space clean and tidy. She carried the heavy, clean water up the stairs and the toilet bucket down. Once in a while, Olga brought some food from her father's small farm and she cooked us a feast. Olga cooked soups and baked Kuchen and cooked all sort of potato dishes. I think her family was glad to get rid of her, a teenager and one less mouth to feed. Besides cooking, Olga helped my mother with the laundry which was done by hand. She had to heat the water for my bath on the stove, my mother could not lift the heavy pail.

The two got along well. Olga loved standing in front of the small mirror to fixing her hair, she combed my hair also and she shared some of her pretty ribbons and bows with me. Mirror, mirror on the wall .... of course we had to get rid of the lice that I brought home from school several times.

She braided my hair and I looked like Gretel without Hansel.

Olga helped getting a school dress for me, I only had one. It was lengthened and stretched for the school year, lengthen the arms, and lengthen the skirt. She helped to knit sweaters and socks and every piece of material was recycled and used over. Shoes were very difficult to come by. If boots were not your size and did not fit anyone in your house hold, holes were cut out in front so the toes would stick out and they would be useful just a bit longer, maybe for another season. If you could find a pair of shoes that were too large, you stuffed a small amount of paper or something else in the front till you grew enough to fit them.

If any material was left from an old shoe, some skilled person used the leather for a small wallet. Every small piece of any kind of material, may it be fabric, wool or leather was used over and over, till it disintegrated. There was not much people could not do. Ingenuity kicked in. I think that's why Germans are so creative.

I started school in Hoechberg, the small village school where we settled in for the next five years. The school was located close to the Church, a good half hour walk from my house. I am not kidding, the school was at the other end of town. Usually I picked up two girl friends on the way and we walked and talked together. One friend, Monika, was always late and I had to wait for her while her mother curled her blond locks with a hot iron heated in the hot coals in the stove. She got "Schiller Locken" (locks), a style of curls named after the famous German poet Johann Schiller.

Monika's mother always asked me "what did you have for dinner today?" (Dinner was served at noon in Germany.) My standard answer was potato soup. I tried to impress her with my healthy diet. I believed potato soup was a hardy meal and the answer to my problem. To my dismay I did not get it very often, since my Mutti's delicate stomach did not tolerate a hardy diet. Due to my mother's stomach ulcers, her diet consisted mostly of goat milk, oat meal and cream of wheat. I wanted to impress my school friend's mother with my healthy meals. Mutti was dependent on a bland diet and I was fed the same. I was so embarrassed to tell about my baby food diet, so potato soup sounded like a good alternative to me. I would have died for potato soup.

My school day started at 1:00 pm. There was a morning shift beginning at 8 p.m. and a shift with afternoon classes. I had the afternoon classes. Saturdays was morning only. Not enough class rooms for all the children since most of the building was damaged. I was taught by nuns, who were very mean to us little kids. They always had a ruler or switch handy to discipline us. They pulled us by the ear and hair and were not afraid to call us bad names. Today, it would be called child abuse. We learned to fire back at the nuns and that would be called disrespectful in today's world. We had to survive and being in survival mode was bred into us children. I learned to look out for myself.

My mother became friendly with the family who lived one floor below us. Emil, his wife Betty and their son Klaus also from Wuerzburg, they shared the good and bad times with us. Betty had a great sense of humor and we laughed a lot. We also sang a lot. We sang songs when at home or when we walked. Looking back now, singing is something satisfying and gratifying. People were singing to forget their misery.

Our new friends, the "Family Emil Reiter", that's what we called them, ate mostly noodles with jam made from the berries. That was their daily meal. Klaus and I picked the berries in the forest. Emil, his father, who had returned very early from the war due to an injury, had to walk to the City (about five miles) every day to "schipp", meaning pushing a broom or shovel to clear the streets from the rubble. Every able bodied human, mostly women (not too many able bodied males around) had to go to the city to help clear the streets from rubble and debris from the bombed-out buildings.

The Allied powers ordered all females between the ages of 15-50 to participate in the postwar cleanup. The women who had to do that job were called "Truemmer Frauen". The old trolley tracks came in handy and were useful to transport stones, bricks and debris on wagons. The streets had to get cleared, stones from buildings where cleaned and washed so they could be used again for new construction. The rebuilding of Germany, including Wuerzburg, started about 1947. My mother was excused since she was sick most of the time.

I will never forget these times, but I don't want to remember them either.

Woman cleaning stones and rubble

My Father Returns

SERVICE DES PRISONNIERS
DE GUERRE

DÉPOT N° 501
DE CHARTRES .

737, 15 frs.

CERTIFICAT DE DÉPOT DE FONDS.

Le Commandant du Dépôt de P.G. certifie que le solde

créditeur du compte particulier du prisonnier de Guerre

(1) *RUPPRECHT, Theo* , N°Mle. *757 036*

s'établit comme suit au moment de son rapatriement:

sept - cent - trente- sept francs 15 cts.

Aligné en solde jusqu'au **31 MAI 1946** inclus.

Avoir en billets de la Banque de France: **31 MAI 1946** 194

(1) Nom et Prénoms) Fait à CHARTRES, le
LE COMMANDANT DU DÉPOT
(timbre humide)

Receipt for small amount of travel money received
from French war prison for trip back to Germany

The village of Hoechberg was not bombed, except some accidental bombs fell on the school and church. We kids played in the streets and it was exciting when an American military caravan came thru. The soldiers gave us gum, sometimes a chocolate bar. What a treat, we loved it. Whatever they gave us or they threw out of the truck window we picked up and made use of it. We collected their cigarette butts and took them back to Emil. He opened the butts, collected the tobacco. He was able to find some very thin paper to roll himself a very thin cigarctte. Than he licked the two ends of paper together, and walla/bingo, he had a cigarette to smoke. How clever was that. In time he managed to get a little handmade gadget/machine, the very thin paper cut to perfect size, and with the left over tobacco from the butts, he rolled new cigarettes every day. Betty and my mother also got one or at least they got to share one. For Klaus and me it was a new job to follow the Army caravans when they rolled thru town and collect their cigarette butts.

Mother and I walked to the city many times to visit my grandparents, my father's family. She always left a note with her in-laws where we can be found if/or when my father returns. We had not heard from my father in very a long time. She also left one of my father's pictures with the local "Red Cross" agency with all possible addresses written on back where we can be found.

Small wooden structures like barracks' started to spring up on the outskirts of the city with limited goods to sell and purchase. We looked in the display windows with very limited supply and I saw a doll, a baby doll wrapped in a piece of cloth as a blanket. I fell in love with that baby and was dying to have it. Since Christmas was only a few month away, my mother bought it for me. With leftover remnants, my mother knitted a little sweater for my baby. A week before Christmas my baby doll disappeared. I could not have lost it, I would not lose it, I was trained to never leave anything of mine behind. So where is it? One evening before the arrival of the Christ child (Christmas), I peeked thru the curtain which my mother had cleverly hung to divide one larger sized room into two tiny rooms, making one room a make-shift kitchen, the other a bedroom. Mutti sat on top of the table, to be closer to the only light in the room. She took the handle of a very small basket, detached it and then attached it to the bottom of the basket to turn it into a cradle. She took some left over material and made a skirt for the cradle, a little pillow and bed cover for my baby. That was my Christmas present under the tree. My doll baby was sleeping in a cradle, my baby was back, I was happy.

It was 1947, we kids were playing outside. It was a warm day maybe summer or early fall, the women were opening the windows to air out the rooms. It was a common thing to do, leaning out the window and watching people walk by or pushing their bicycle up the hill where we lived. A very skinny man was walking up the hill pushing his bicycle. Betty, our neighbor, spotted him first and shouted, "Theo is coming, Theo is coming, I recognize him, that is Theo walking up the hill". Theo, my father. He walked on foot all the way from Saint Nazaire, France, the war prison where he was held in for several years. My mother had heard thru word of mouth that he could be detained in a French prison camp north of Paris, but nothing was ever confirmed. He was released in 1947. Only if a prisoner was sick, he would be released. Having NO teeth was considered being sick. (You could not eat, obviously) Most of the prisoners had their teeth pulled and not by a dentist either. That was considered sick enough to be released.

My father had stopped by my grandparent's house in Wuerzburg, they provided him with our whereabouts in Hoechberg. He found an old bicycle in the shed and soon he was on this way to Hoechberg. Oh, I was so happy to see him even so I could not recognize him. My Renatele, (a name of endearment) he yelled out loud. It was good to have my Vati back.

My mother and father had a difficult time re-connecting after so many years apart. Olga was let go, my Vati moved in and was now able to help with the daily chores. I had missed him so much. Of course I only saw him on his vacations and not at all since 1943/44.

The two of us got along well, I think I was more like him. He always was proud of me the way I was and offered lots of adorations. He was happy to see us and again I was his "Huepferle". He had so many nick-names for me. He was never tired or idle and he was very handy to have around. He bounced me on his knees like I was still his baby, catching up with the time he had missed with me.

Vati managed to find work in the city shortly after his return from war prison in France. Before he could start any job or employment, he had to be "De-Nazified". It had something to do with National Socialism. He had to go to court with witnesses and proof that he never was a Nazi, that he did not belong to the SS Party. Mutti and I went along to the court to show that he was a good family man. After he was DE-Nazified and cleared, he got a job right away. Vati also managed to get new teeth, he had a relative who was a dental technician.

My father managed to be put on the list for his old job with the Finanzamt, but first it had to be re-build. It was not till 1950 till we were allocated an apartment in Wuerzburg. Buildings had to be build and re-built. In the meantime he traveled to the city by bicycle every day. I heard my parents talk about the "Denazification –process" and they talked about never ever to join any political group or organization anywhere. It became a lesson for me. I never joined or belonged to any organization except the church choir. I figured that was safe enough and would not create any recourses later in life.

One day a letter arrived from a woman in France addressed to my father. This letter changed everything.

It happened a lot in those days, Soldiers fighting a war in another country for so many years, they found comfort in another woman's arms. My father had a "fling" with a French woman and my mother had a difficult time accepting his infidelity. The question was put to me, "Who do you want to live with?" I was devastated. So happy to have my father back but I also loved my mother deeply. No decision was made and my mother had a very difficult time dealing with any of it. No forgiveness on her part, just a lot of fighting and screaming. Remember, after I was born father promised my mother no more childbearing for her. He almost lost her when she gave birth to me. I think my father had several "flings" over the years, but he always provided for us and never stopped loving us. I was his pride and joy and I kept worrying that they would separate. But they stayed together, sometimes under very difficult situations and arguing a lot. What was my mother to do, no education, no job, no income, sick most of the time and housing was just about nonexistent. It was difficult enough to find one apartment for the three of us.

After I left for America life was better for my parents, they actually got along better. They were amicable and content with each other and satisfied with their lives in their later years.

We had lived in Hoechberg in this small apartment for five years till 1951. It was a difficult time for my family to live in such tiny quarters without facilities. Most every day my father walked to the nearby woods to use as a make-shift outhouse, while my mother and I still used the bucket. We collected leaves from bushes to use as toilet paper. Paper products were non-existent. Everybody did it the same way. There was only one bathroom in the two story house for four families. My father refused to share the same facilities with everybody in the house. Mutti and I shared the bucket.

I don't think there was a proper septic system, you could tell by the smell.

We took a bath once a week. My father carried the water upstairs in buckets, then it was heated on the coal/wood stove. We had a large wash tub. I got washed first, than my mother and my father was last in line since he was the biggest and most likely the dirtiest. I do like to mention so, we washed our bodies every day and soap was some home-made concoction.

I started school in an old school building next to the only church in town. The cemetery was next to the church and both were a good place to play in. My school girl friends (boys and girls were always separated) and I walked thru the cemetery every day. School was either from 8 am till 12 or from 1- 4 pm. On Saturdays only morning classes were scheduled, no classes in the afternoon. Too many pupils and not enough class room space. I got a book satchel which I carried on my back, a leather backpack filled with a framed slate board and several very skinny, long slate pencils called Griffel. I could write on my small blackboard with the Griffel, than used a little wet sponge to wipe the tablet clean. We learned how to write the alphabet, first in block letters and then cursive. We practice our letters and numbers continuously. There were 45 pupils in one class room.

Our teachers were Nuns and if we did not behave and/or cooperate we either had to stand in the corner facing the corner. The Nuns also pulled out the switch and we had to hold out our hands. She pulled us by the ear or hair, there was no mercy. I think all their frustration was let out on us children.

Each child had to bring a tin pot/container to school to collect breakfast, mostly oatmeal, a paste not edible or meant for human consumption. Most of the kids hated it, unless some kakau was added. After school we walked into the church and dumped the oatmeal on the seat of the confession stand/booth or we climbed the steps to the Kanzel where the sermon was read from and emptied our porridge. We never got caught. We thought of all sorts of mischievous things to do.

We had no play grounds or organized sports, we played in the streets and/or harassed the people. We had no toys. No board games or card games. To this day I don't like to play board games or cards, I never had any as a kid, so I am not used to that. I prefer to be creative and accomplish something.

I liked to walk in the forest and meadows. We had beautiful meadows with small brooks and clear waters, our forests were like swept clean. Not a twig was laying on the ground, the forests where picked clean for firewood and kindling. We watched bad people hide in the forest, the Gypsies wandered thru the forests from one town to the next, escaping from the Russians and making their way from one country to the next. They never walked on the streets, always thru the forest so they would not be noticed or seen. Undesirables would be hiding in the forest also.

Another fun thing to do was watch the shepherds with their sheep. The shepherd pulled a small covered wagon by hand. He always had a herd dog and tended to a large herd of sheep. The cart stored a mattress which became his bed. He also carried a pot and a frying pan, and he made a fire to cook his meal. Usually the shepherd was a loner, a weird guy. We girls were told to stay away from him, but we did not obey the rules. We chased him till we caught up with him, talked to him and hung out until he moved on. He always had interesting stories to tell, a world of information he shared with us. We teased him and enjoyed playing tricks on him.

During the five years we lived in Hoechberg, the young men from the community cleared a field and started to played soccer. The boys cut some trees and made benches to sit on and soon on Sundays we watched soccer games. The neighboring villages started their own teams and before long we could watch the teams play each other. We did not think anything of it to walk five miles one way to watch our team play. After all we had nothing better to do than to get in trouble.

In third grade, being nine years old, I made my 1st communion. It was March, still quite cold being the end of winter. Tante Marga made a lovely white dress for me, another friend provided me with a coat made from a white rabbit skin. The coat barely covered my fanny, (must have been a small animal, I certainly did not have a big butt)) it was on the short side. Mutti thought it was lovely and I needed to fit into it, come rain or high water. Well, the nuns who were my teachers told my mother this coat did not fit me properly, it needs to be longer and has to cover my butt. My mother let her have it and told her in so many words if you don't like my daughter's coat you better come up with a different one for her. My daughter is going to wear this coat and that was the end. I was proud to have a white rabbit coat and happy to wear it.

I got to carry a huge candle with the date of my birth and the date of my first communion carved in the wax, I think the candle was larger than I, we had a really big First Communion Celebration, the first celebration I remember.

First Communion Celebration

Vati managed to get some meat from one of the farmers and wine was always available. We had a real festive get-together with relatives who lived in the area and could make the trip on foot. Nobody had a vehicle and public transportation did not exist. The lucky ones had a bicycle. First communion was a big deal in our catholic community. It was the first celebration that I attended. After all, we had nothing to celebrate in the past years.

The black market was a big illegal business by that time and people were trading back and forth. It was against the law to trade on the black market but people did it anyway. Several weeks of jail time could be your punishment if caught. Cigarettes were high in demand and if you could get any from the American Soldiers you were in pretty good shape. Uncle Julius always helped out with a few extra cigars.

We had very little money. The small amount we had was not worth anything and there was nothing to purchase any way. Most people were trading. You give me two eggs and 1 give you some cigarettes. Jewelry was also a very important trading object for larger items. Small pieces of jewelry were very good to own, you could get a whole loaf of bread for a small ring.

People had sewn jewelry into their coat and the hem of their dresses to keep their valuables safe.

By summer of 1948 all bank accounts were closed by the government. Every person, including every child was allowed to exchange 600 RM (Reichs Mark) and receive 40 DM (Deutsch Marks). Everybody started out fresh with very little cash. It was called "Ent-Waehrung". Translated the amount into US currency, may be $10.

Those five years after the war were the worst year of my young life.

We all were so poor, but not without hope. Since we all were poor, it did not feel like poor.

Nobody had anything and we were in survival mode.

The German motto was "NIE WIEDER" - "NEVER AGAIN" will Germany be involved in a war.

Germany was scarred forever by Adolf Hitler and the Holocaust

Back In Wuerzburg - 1950

We had lived in Hoechberg for five long and very difficult years. In 1951 an apartment became available for us thru my father's work. It was a good size apartment (or so it appeared to us) on the fourth floor under the roof or you may call it under the attic. We were happy to move back to the city. All of our evacuated relatives and friends tried to move back to Wuerzburg as soon as possible, at heart we always remained City folks.

I continued basic school in the Pestalozzi school, a good half hour walk each way (and that's for real) from Ludwig Strasse. I stayed there for two more years till I was able to qualify for higher education and transferred to a Middle Schule which is above the basic school. I only had a 15 minute walk to "Mozart Schule" which offered different classes, including a foreign language. Students had to choose the English language as our primary foreign language, since we were occupied by the Americans. French was offered as a second foreign language. Mandatory subject also were cooking and house-keeping. That was fun. I loved baking, beating up the yeast dough. Shorthand, typing and music, one of my better subject. Sports was low on the list, one hour per week. One's a year the students went to the "Sports Platz", mostly for recreation, fun and competition.

I made new friends immediately and my life started to improve. Mutti signed me up for private ballet lessons, dancing was my dream.

I had great interest in music and was allowed to continue taking accordion lessons, which I had started in Hoechberg. My request for a piano fell on deaf ears, we did not have the space or the money for such luxurious purchases.

My father continued to work for the Government. He again was employed by the Finanzamt, the Internal Revenue Service. We continued living on Ludwig Strasse, just like before the war. It is an extra wide street (or so it seemed at the time) with wide sidewalks, mostly office buildings, no commercial stores. Vati was in charge of the motor cars and garage, being part of the Finanzamt. He also was working as a land Assessor in the same office, surveying lands in the surrounding areas of Wuerzburg. He considered his job a secure position with health insurance and a good retirement. Healthcare was "free" for all. I am sure he paid for it somehow. A certain percentage was deducted from every person's paycheck to cover and pay for health insurance. This system worked well, we never paid for a doctor's visit or hospital stay or any of my mother's medications.

When we moved back to the apartment in the City, my mother reclaimed the oil paintings. They were stored for many years at Uncle Julius's house after they were rescued from the rubble and under the Brickets (coals) in our basement, their hiding place. My parents took them to an art dealer for evaluation, probably to sell. We needed money to start life over.

The art dealer informed my parents that these paintings are registered with the German Art Gallery and are quite valuable and not to sell them. So, the paintings were professionally cleaned (from the coals, dust and dirt) and my parents hung them in their living room. After my mother passed in 1994 I had the paintings shipped to the USA and they are now displayed in my living room. I was never able to find out where the paintings are registered. I would have liked to accomplish that on one of my many visits back to Germany. Unfortunately I procrastinated and never completed that task.

My Vati had promised my mother he would buy her a new bedroom set when we moved back to the city. Remember, there were no stores anywhere. The black market was in full bloom. One day, after my father's work day was finished, we drove to a small village called Ochsenfurt, located only several miles from Wuerzburg. My father had found a make shift furniture store. The furniture for sale were to be viewed in a barn that was fixed up as a warehouse. Connections were needed to find such desirable item. I am sure several boxes of cigars were involved in the trade and purchase.

The oak bedroom set, including two beds, two night stands, large dresser with mirror and a large wardrobe for our clothes; large enough so I could hide in it. It was brand new and beautiful and soon delivered to our new apartment. Vati placed a box of chocolates on the night table for my Mutti. I thought this was such a sweet thing for him to do. He was always thoughtful and generous. We did not have many furniture, we accumulated our furniture piece by piece. Since we only bought with cash, it took us years to furnish the apartment. That was the way it was done in those days. I remember my mother complaining, "this is the second time I have to furnish an apartment and buy everything new". She was sad all her beautiful furniture and wedding presents (she had buried a few under the coals to later retrieve them) where gone. It was difficult for everybody to lose all their belongings in bombing strikes and find no replacements available, many items were priceless.

Father's biggest hobby and interests were automobiles. He always was a member of the ADAC club, before the war and after. ADAC means Allgemeiner Deutscher Automobile Club. (maybe General Automobile Club) It is an automobile club, somewhat exclusive at that time since the average person did not own an automobile. Some folks were members who did not even own a car but were working to acquiring such a luxury item.

Not that we could afford a car, but we never were without one. Father collected a part here and there and soon he was able to build his own car. His brother, my uncle Willy owned an upholstery business and he re-upholstered old seats for us with leftover material and remnants and the inside looked beautiful. Soon we had a car painted yellow and black. We called it Biene, meaning Bee. Maybe it was buzzing and humming like a bee.

My father was voted to head up the entertainment committee of his ADAC club and he was happy to be in charge of parties and get-to-gathers for the organization.

One of his project every year was to head up and organized several trips for the "Weisen Kinder". Those were the many orphaned children living in institutions. There were many "Heime" around the Wuerzburg area.

He arranged the annual Easter Egg Hunt. The children got to ride in a private automobile, most of them had never ridden in a car. They were served a nice meal in a restaurant. Then came the Easter egg hunt. A large Easter bunny (my father) ran thru the meadows and all the kids started chasing the bunny. After the hunt we went to a restaurant, musicians played the zither, harmonica and accordion and we all danced the waltzes and polkas. Later on in the afternoon delicious desserts were served. The "Weisen Kinder" enjoyed their outing and had a special time. Then back to the City and the kids were dropped off at the orphanage.

For Christmas, my father arranged the same style party as we enjoyed for Easter, for the orphaned children. In early December Vati dressed up to become St. Nick. Again the Children were served dinner, cookies and cake and each child received a gift. Vati had so much fun organizing these functions and enjoyed all the success for the ADAC club. After all, HE was the head of the "entertainment committee".

Easter bunny

St. Nick

My family had fun with our automobile, took many vacation trips over the next years. The Vor-Alpen or "Allgaeu" as it is called in Bavaria, southern Germany, were my father's favorite destination. He knew the name of every town, lake and especially the mountains. We never visited North Germany, he was drawn to the Bavarian lifestyle.

Most every Sunday we took my Omi (my mother's Mom) with us for a ride. She got to sit in the front seat. We stopped for a bite to eat and then a walk in the country side. I spent every Sunday with my parents, weekends were family time and we did things together. Sometimes a girlfriend could come along.

At age 16 in 1955 I graduated from Mozart Schule but almost flunked my English course. It was my worst subject. It was the required foreign language, since we were occupied by Americans and lived in the American Zone. At that time I told myself I will never ever need the English language. So, why should I learn this language? How different life turned out!

My two Aunts offered to send me to fashion school in Muenchen but my father did not like the idea. So far away and all alone, strange people! No, no, you need your family! You do not need more or higher education, you are a girl and you will get married. Final words from my father.

I continued my education in the "Berufs Schule", a business school where I had to attend one day of school every week while I also worked. Vati had found me a job thru some of his connections. I started as an apprentice to become an "Industrie Kaufmann". University is only for serious students who want to be doctors and engineers, etc., it was not for me, I guess I was not serious enough. Vati kept telling me, "you are a girl, you will get married soon and become a Hausfrau and mother". In Germany you have trade-schools available.

My job as an apprentice was in one of Wurzburg's two breweries called "Wuerzburger Buerger Braeu", a very large business and very competitive with the world famous "Wuerzburger Hofbraeu". I was hired to be an apprentice in the bookkeeping department, accounting, including accounts payable and receiving, anything to do with the business part of the brewery. I did shorthand and typing for the "Herr Director". Every morning I was handed an attaché case filled with cash to go to the bank to make the previous day's cash collections and deposits. I was transporting thousands of Deutsch Marks every day.

I took the trolley to the city and walked the rest of the way to the bank. No protection, no guard and nobody ever attempted to rob me.

I was told by my parents that I have a good future there working for the brewery after completing my three years apprenticeship. After two years I left the job.

It was in the middle of winter and I was on my daily walk to the bank. It was brutally cold. I was wearing a dress, a coat and the very fashionable nylon stockings. The "Herr Director" made the rules, females were not allowed to wear anything but dresses and skirts, no long pants for woman. Needless to say I was freezing my buns off. My uncle Julius always kept an eye out for me, (I was his favorite niece) he spotted me walking on the street not being properly dressed in his opinion, on a brutally cold winter day. I told him that "Herr Director" ordered (and I mean ordered, he ordered everyone around, the boss man) for females to wear dresses or skirts only, while working at his office. My uncle rang the "Herr Director" and informed him his niece could not walk outdoors in the middle of a brutally cold winter day and risk frost bite. Immediately the rules for me were changed. I was allowed to wear slacks when I was on my daily walks and run errands. Uncle Julius had a special authority since he was a very successful business man and very large in stature. He also told me to remember his rule. "If you are cold, you're either poor or stupid and since you are not poor you must be stupid". Somehow this stuck with me and as of today I still remembered this statement.

Occasionally Uncle Julius slipped me a chocolate bar and ones he bought me a small dog. He traded a box of cigars for a puppy. I definitely was his favorite niece.

In my father's homemade car Mutti and I got to go on rides. The original car was a DKW, a "Deutscher Kraft Wagen" which later on was called "Audi". It was so exiting, the car was newly painted and sparkled. Sundays was family day and Vati took the car out of the garage to show it off. My grandmother sat in the passenger seat while my mother and I were in the back seat. If someone else came along, they had to sit in the back seat also. No seat belts, no rules, no regulations. Sometimes we were squeezed in like sardines in a can. "A bad ride is better than a good walk", that was my mother's philosophy. My father had a different opinion. If it rained on a Sunday and my mother had plans to go somewhere, we had to take the trolley. We could get wet, but not the car. After every ride the car was washed and if by misfortune the car got caught in a rain shower it had to be rinsed off and polished. That car was my father's pride and joy.

As soon as we had moved back to Wuerzburg I was able to take ballet lessons. Mother enrolled me in ballet school, the lessons being instructed by an elderly ballerina who had escaped from Russia. She opened a small ballet school to earn her living teaching dance. It was strictly ballet, no other kind of dance. I loved to dance. I loved the music and the different moves we learned. I did toe/point dancing which gave us students bloody toes for the first few months.

Once a year we got to perform on stage. That was the highlight for our yearlong dance practice. I loved it, but I was nervous and had stage fright. Two of my best friends from school also took lessons and with these two friends by my side I managed to perform. I continued and enjoyed the dance classes till I was about 15 years old when I had to have an emergency appendectomy. I was in hospital for nine days and had to stop dancing for six months. After the long recovery period I was out of practice and soon other interests occupied my time. I was in my last year of school and had to prepare for my future, (making something of myself), that's what they called it. Boys started to notice me and they whistled when I walked by. I crossed the street not to be noticed.

My cousin Helga who was two years older, needed someone to hang out with, she chose me. We hung out together, we were cousins and best pals. Maybe more like sisters, we had a strong bond. On Sundays we went to church together, sometimes we skipped it. However we told my grandmother that we attended church. It was a huge City church and you could not find anybody if you wanted too. After the service we had a special corner outside where we would meet up with our Oma. She always gave each of us one Deutsche Mark (a German coin) for going to Church. Anyway, we made sure we were at the corner at the right time so we would get our coins.

Quite frequently we missed church service but we never missed to be at the corner at the expected time. Now we could purchase an Italian ice-cream cone or maybe two.

Many Italians had fled Italy during and after the war and ended up settling in Germany. The Italians were known for making delicious ice-cream and also introduced Pizza to their newly selected country. In the winter months they closed up shop, went back to Italy and returned back to Germany in the spring time.

One early spring day this young Italian ice-cream shop owner came to our apartment, rang the doorbell and while standing in the doorway, asked my Mutti for my hand in marriage. He brought both of us beautiful scarfs, (I still have mine). I was about 16 years old and never saw this man other than buying ice-cream cones from him thru the walk-up window. His name was Alberto and his home town was Cortina d'Ampezzo. He was short and slim and did not come close to what I had imagined for my future husband. He definitely was not my type. My first proposal, ha ha. My mother was upset, I had to laugh but at the same time was flattered that he had noticed me.

Helga and I met some boys who were students at the University, they were from Hamburg, North Germany. We became their tour guides and we showed off our beautiful city to them. We also met boys when we took a dance class, almost a requirement for teenagers in Germany. It was just about the only opportunity to meet someone of the opposite sex. I never went to school with boys or had any brothers who would bring a boy home.

Ballroom dancing, so much fun. I was able to show off the moves I had learned in ballet class. We learned to waltz, did the fox trot and loved to tango. Good manners were also in high order, as if we did not know that already; it was expected and very important to act appropriately. We made new friends there. Two boys, friends and both of their parents owned bakeries and coffee shops; these young men were working in their parent's businesses. We had fun together but no further interests.

Our parents told us, these boys are good marriage material and we could have a good life if we would pursue a relationship. Our parents encouraged us to hang out with these guys. So we tried again, went for a few more walks on Sunday afternoons but nothing clicked. I was sixteen, but could not see myself with any of these boys. Helga was two years older and that was a different situation, I had to accompany her as a chaperone. We hooked our arms together and walked, walked, walked and talked, talked, talked like teenage girls do. We decided to send these "very appropriate boys", so called marriage material, off on their happy way.

Getting Married

I became a member of a local Jazz Club. Several young people were getting together with interest in music, especially Jazz. After a short while our German Club was invited by the American Jazz Club, to listen and visit with their musicians. Some American jazz musicians were performing. How exciting. It was in a catacomb style Cellar, empty wooden wine crates to sit on, very rustic. I was hooked. After a few visits, the pianist showed some special interest in me. I was fascinated and mesmerized with the music. At almost 17 I fell in love and my parents came close to having a stroke. An American, a soldier and musician - impossible. Well, the more they were against it, the better I liked him.

I don't know what I liked better, him or his ability to play the piano. Maybe he could teach me how to play the piano. I already knew how to play the accordion, not very well, but it was a keyboard. I had taken lessons when we lived in Hoechberg. Vati had bought a beautiful Hohner instrument for me, which after years of practice ended up sitting in a corner. I did not like to carry the instrument around, it was so heavy. I believe it hurt my back by doing so and I have been suffering from curvature of the spine ever since. I much rather would have had a Klavier, an up-right piano.

Besides his musical abilities this young US soldier was 6'2" tall, slim and handsome. What more could I ask for? I fell in love! It was just one of those things, just one of those fabulous things....

Renata and Doug

To the great disappointment of my parents, a courtship started. It was a very difficult time dating an American soldier, but we made it work. When we met for a date, he always smelled freshly showered and soon I was hooked on his "Old Spice" aftershave lotion, which was his favorite.

That special aftershave/cologne will always be associated with him.

He also was a smoker which looked very sophisticated at the time. He offered me my first cigarette, I literally choked on it. It was also my last cigarette, which was a good thing for me. Of course I did not realize it at that at time, since I was totally embarrassed with the coughing attack I experienced.

I loved music and this was our common denominator. Doug bought me records which I played on my little record player. Ella

Fitzgerald, Sarah Vaughn, my favorites. I was in heaven. He played the piano in the club and I was humming along. He played effortlessly, so much talent and feelings. Doug was kind of shy but had no problems to put all his feelings into music. For the first time I heard the words progressive Jazz, improvise and jam session. I was hooked.

Doug asked me to marry him on New Year's Eve 1957 and the wedding followed in April, 1958. My parents were totally against this union, I was their only child. However, they finally approved and after many years I think I figured out why they approved. My mother's Cousin Doris, also an only child and 15 years my senior, had fallen in love with a fellow the parents did not approve of. She was not allowed to marry him and ended up with a broken heart and committed suicide. Certainly my parents did not want me to take that route. They did not want that tragedy for their daughter.

They gave their blessing.

My parents came to accept Douglas; he was a good person. Their only objection was for me to be moving to another country. This broke their hearts.

We had a lovely wedding ceremony in the American Episcopalian Church. Doug was Episcopalian and I was Catholic but I did not practice the religion. I saw too much cruelty and destruction, death and misery, including unfairness during my short life. The Catholic Church excommunicated me, since I refused to sign the proper papers for my unborn children to be raised in the Catholic Church. I thought I should be able to make that decision without the church telling me what to do.

My soon to be mother-in-law flew to Germany to attend the wedding, also to check out if I was suitable and appropriate for her only child. She turned out to be a woman "in charge" and ran the show. I began to understand why her only son and my future husband enlisted in the military.

Doug's father would not make the trip, he was afraid to fly and could not be away from his animals for more than a day. I am sure he enjoyed his time alone.

Tante Marga had designed and made a spectacular wedding dress for me, the newest style and lots of special lace. The dress was my wedding present from her. Cousin Helga served as my maid of honor, a custom we don't recognize in Germany. My mother-in-law organized the whole ceremony, my parents were in charge of the celebration/ party that was held at their apartment. Doug invited all of the Army band to our wedding reception, about 50 musicians in dress uniform and instruments in hand, showed up. The dance band was complete.

And what a party it was.

One of my wedding pics 1958 with my mother-law

The song popular at the time was "Bridge on the River Kwai". We had a parade on the street and it was an unforgettable celebration. My Uncle Hans, Helga's father was found with a bottle of Whiskey (I don't think he knew what he was drinking, or so we all wanted to believe) sitting in a corner happy as a lark. All my aunts (I had quite a few on my father's side), had shown up early in the morning to help with the cooking and baking, Doug provided whiskey and wine and it was an unforgettable event. My relatives had never seen such a party before, and neither had I.

Our wedding night we spent at a nice Hotel Garni (a hotel without food service) within walking distance from my parent's home. Once settled in the hotel room, I realized I had not eaten all day. I sent my new husband back to my parent's apartment to collect some food. By the time he returned, I was sound asleep. No love making that night. I slept thru my wedding night. Too much of a good thing, plus my new mother-in-law slept in the room next door which was a bit of an uncomfortable situation. She tagged along every move we made. Three days after the wedding reality set in. What happened and what did I do? All the excitement was great fun but now I am married?

The honeymoon was short or I should say non-existent. The 10th Division Band including my new husband, was shipped back to the United States at the end of April 1958. We were married on April 20th. Since I did not have a Visa, I could not go. We were separated for six months till my papers were finalized and I was able to travel to the USA in October 1958.

I had quit my job at the brewery that spring and with my improved English language skills I got a job at the American Military Hospital in Wuerzburg as a switchboard operator. It paid well, more than twice the amount of money than the brewery paid for being an apprentice, and I had the opportunity to practice and speak English.

And I thought I never needed to learn that English language!

I had a lovely summer that year, made many friends at the hospital and I matured some. I met a young man who worked at the hospital, he was smitten with me and promised me the world. I liked him a lot, but I was married. By the end of summer I was doubtful of my decision to get married at such an early age and had committed moving to America. My mother told me: you made your bed, now you will lay in it. Amen! You are not going to embarrass me.

During the summer my dowry was put together and the American military packed all my wedding presents and mementos into huge shipping crates to be shipped to America. Six gigantic containers/ boxes, filled to the rim. My whole life was in those boxes.

PART 2

MY NEW LIFE

Picture of our wedding

In October 1958 after physicals, many immunizations and all my paperwork in order, I flew to my new country. I still have the certificate which reads, "TWA Transatlantic Flight – Frankfurt to New York, 25th of October 1958". My parents gave me a gold trinket to wear on a necklace, engraved with the date of my departure. They took me to the airport. The plane I was to fly on was sitting on the tarmac and a long walking distance from where we said good bye. I kissed them both, walked away, never turned around. I knew, tears were flowing down their faces and mine too; what did I do to them? How could I be so selfish? My parents did everything for me. This was for real, no turning back now.

It was a very long flight, like 18 hours on a military propeller plane, with a landing in Ireland to re-fuel. Our next stop was Iceland for breakfast. All I remember, we walked in the bitter cold from the plane to a Mess Hall to eat breakfast. It was so terribly cold, none of the passengers had proper clothing. Strong ice-cold winds and snow was blowing on the tarmac.

After breakfast we were on our way to the USA.

I arrived late afternoon on a Friday in Fort Dix, NJ. The Army administration offices were about to close for the weekend and would not process my paperwork that late in the day. I was told I had to spend the weekend on the Army base. It was horrible, I did not know anything, I was out of my comfort zone in a new country, 3000 miles from home. Ordering food in the cafeteria was new and an ordeal for me, every soldier was watching me and hoping I was not picking up their favorite food. I just did not belong. I'd rather starve than stand in line. Should I smile or cry?

I met a young German woman, maybe a few years older than I who was returning to Germany. She had noticed my discomfort and offered her help. Her stay in the US lasted only three months. She had decided this new country was not for her. I got scared. She was also stuck for the weekend and we agreed to room together for the next two nights. Without her I probably would have returned to Germany on the next flight, which would have been the following Monday.

The paper work and process continued Monday morning. I stood in line again and when it was my turn, the Sargent informed me they have to call my husband in Georgia and ask him if he still wanted me to come. He was serious. How insulting. If my husband's answer would have been NO, I would have been shipped back to Germany immediately. Well, good for him that he agreed to receive me and I began my flight to Columbus, GA, just outside Ft. Benning,

Doug was very happy to see me, welcoming me with open arms. I was exhausted, tired and scared. My new country, especially the State of Georgia did not make a good impression on me. The landscape was flat and the earth was red and I saw more car dealerships with little flags blowing in the wind on one street than the whole city of Wuerzburg all together had to show for.

My husband had purchased a one story Ranch style house for us, he wanted to surprise me. It was located at 2849 Grant Road, Columbus, GA. 1000 square foot, two bedroom, one bath. The house was off base, located in a residential neighborhood. He wanted to surprise me with a house. He also had purchased all the furniture. He meant well but put us in a lot of debt. The house had a very large living room, so he also had to purchase a huge carpet to cover the hardwood floors. Now we need a vacuum cleaner he announced, and NO, you cannot sweep the carpet with a broom. I was going to sweep the dirt to each side and that would work. Well, that did not work. I just did not want to spend money we did not have, especially since I was not contributing at all. Both our intentions were good but I was trying to keep the debt load down.

From a door to door salesman we purchased an Electrolux vacuum cleaner which we could not afford. But only in America can you buy things without money. The American lifestyle started with monthly payments and a big debt load, something I was not used too.

My parents paid cash for everything, if they did not have the money, we did not purchase. My financial independence was gone, we had no money, we only had bills. Car payment, insurance, mortgage, furniture, appliances, and the list went one. Wages for a soldier in the military were fairly low, which I learned quickly. However there were benefits, like health insurance, housing allotment and others.

Doug was able to play dance gigs every weekend to make extra dollars so we could survive. I spent a lot of time by myself, writing letters to my parents, hundreds of letters. I did not want for them to know how homesick I was, so I wrote about all kinds of beautiful things that I dreamed of.

I asked Doug if I could have a bicycle. I would just love to be mobile and ride around. The answer was no. Only schoolchildren ride bikes in this country I was told, so I was stuck. It was not proper for a young white woman to walk, run or exercise by herself, so that idea was out.

Doug was becoming an accomplished jazz musician and it seemed if he was not at work playing in the Army band he was playing in clubs.

I did not have a job to occupy myself with, I did not have any skills to work in my new country, no transportation. I developed a daily routine, visiting my neighbor's black "help". I enjoyed talking with the maids, mostly women older than I. It was difficult to understanding their slang, but they had a lot to complain about and it was very entertaining.

The residential neighborhood we lived in had big yards with lots of pine trees and all our neighbors had colored maids to take care of their children, clean the house, feed the children and fix supper. When the lady of the house came home from her cushy job (they all had easy jobs, like answering the phone at a business, or being some sort of receptionist), the "lady" took the maid home and then returned to sit down to a prepared meal.

Many times we were invited to chicken BBQ's and enjoyed an evening meal at our very friendly neighbors. They were good folks and meant well. Just different. But they never let us forget that "we" were Yankees. The English language along with the southern slang was difficult to understand. My "Oxford style" English that I had learned in school did not fit in with the southern dialect or slang.

My style of clothing did not fit in either with what the young people wore in Georgia. Wide, full skirts, socks and blouses with rolled up sleeves was the style here.

My husband had many black musician friends being in the Army band. We enjoyed inviting his friends and band members to our house for a visit, to listen to music or a jam session. However, we had to wait till it was dark and draw all the curtains and blinds so nobody could look inside. The neighbors would have send the KuKlux-Klan to set our house on fire and hung us from the next tree, had they seen we were entertaining friends of color. All so different, segregation was in full swing and somewhat scary. The guys liked to jam and listen to records on our new record player. The record player was rather large and had huge speakers. Music was our passion and enjoyment and I became very familiar with Jazz and the Blues and big sound bands like the Glen Miller Band. I could get myself lost in the sound of music.

Life went on in Georgia for two years and I experienced "Life in the Deep South". Coming from a highly cultured country with theaters and concert halls, city life and somewhat more sophisticated people, I felt like I was on another planet. Well, not quite, but another continent.

One of our neighbors owned coonhounds and he went hunting

for raccoons and other small animals, shooting at everything that moved and he did that mostly at night. Since we lived in a residential neighborhood and not on the Army base, all our neighbors were white locals, southern folks, not military. I had a hard time understanding the southern slang, life just was not easy for me in these United States. Oh, how I missed my parents, I was so homesick.

On Sundays, Doug taught me how to cook. I was totally ignorant as far as cooking was concerned, or for that matter, anything else. I was not prepared to live in this country, or prepared to live the American life style.

I did not know how to boil water, never had to do any work in the kitchen. Never heard of a measuring cup. In Germany we use the metric system, we weigh flour and sugar on a scale. We measure in grams and Pfund, (pounds) or Kilograms. A German pound is 500 grams, American pound is 450 grams. The cooking classes I had taking when I attended Mozart Schule, did not help much. Even the flour was of a different consistency in my new country. Milk was sold in big gallon jugs, largest milk container in Germany was a liter and we took our own bottle or can to the store.

I did not know of catsup or other American favorite condiments, or the local favorite foods. The common flavorings in my days were, salt, pepper, vinegar and oil, also mustard very popular. Mayonnaise was always homemade and a delicacy, being used rarely. The favorite bread here was "Wonder Bread". Absolutely no comparison to the hardy, very dark bread I was used to eating. Sweet potatoes, never heard of it. A scary thought. How can anybody eat sweet potatoes? Corn was only for the cows in Germany.

Doug purchased a simple cook book that showed colored pictures of every meal. We started to cook together, every weekend a different meal. May it be meat loaf, beef stew or beef Stroganoff, Chili Con

Carne, I had never heard of any of them. We did chicken on the grill, also new to me. One time we fixed a duck in the oven. We had a great time cooking together and I learned it all very fast.

Baking was also very different. I did not know what degrees were. I was used to "low, and high and you figured out the in-between.

Never heard of a pie, so very popular here in the US. In Germany, we had wonderful breads, delicious Kuchen, Torten and bake goods, cookies were only baked for Christmas. They were a specialty.

Doug was a very good cook and enjoyed showing off his skills and all his favorite foods. Under his supervision I learned quickly. One Sunday afternoon we had some friends over for dinner. We served Spaghetti with sauce and meat balls, a favorite for all. I was thinking "that's why people like this country, the food is really tasty".

Shopping in the commissary was so different from the small grocery stores I was used to. I did not know what the brand names were or recognized packaging or could even identify items on the shelves. Again, I felt lost and disappointed.

On payday, the main trip was to the commissary to shop for all the staples for the rest of month. Meat and other certain items were put in the freezer. (I never heard of a freezer before). Quite a difference from shopping each day for one day at a time. I felt like a child having to learn everything from the very beginning. Very scary, but I learned fast.

One of the first times Doug took me out to a nice restaurant in Columbus, it turned out to be another lesson. I had a real hankering for a beer, so I ordered one with my meal. The waitress set the glass in front of me and I took a large sip. It was root beer. I spit it out with gusto and it went all over. What was this horrible new taste? It tasted like bad medicine or worse. From that day forward, root beer was never on my menu. The waitress also told me I could not have an alcoholic drink, a real beer. I was not of legal age which at that time in Georgia was 21. Who ever heard of that? I have been drinking beer since I was a small child and in small amounts at the dinner table and now I was told I was not old enough to drink a beer. It was humiliating.

We started to go swimming in a man-made lake. There are many man-made lakes in Georgia, but very few natural lakes. The only swimsuit I owned was a red one and by today's standards very conservative. It was a two piece bathing suit, and NOT a bikini. I had a Kim Novak style haircut and every male, mostly soldiers and their female companions or wives stared at me and it made me very uncomfortable. I figured, either I look very good or very bad, anyway, the red swim suit drew a lot of attention. I did not handle this attention well at my age. I was insecure and again felt unattractive and I did not fit in. My husband did not mind at all that I was getting attention, he straddled along like a peacock.

Since I did not have the money to buy a different suit, we did not go back to the lake.

My fashionable clothes which I brought from Germany, were different than what the girls wore here. In style were "bobby" sox and blouses with rolled up sleeves. Full "Poodle skirts" were the in- thing. I had never considered myself to be good looking, to be a beauty, especially after listening to my aunts' opinion. Always more improvement was needed and required according to their opinion, so I became shy and felt unattractive. I had no confidence in myself.

In Germany it is not customary to praise someone, people always criticized me so I would improve myself. Much later I learned, in the USA it's just the opposite. You praise people so they improve themselves. People are praised here if they are not good or talented, especially young children. "Oh, the picture you drew is beautiful" or "you did such a good job" even if it is ugly and they did a poor job. My Aunts didn't think anything of it to call me unattractive. So, I always worked on improving myself, I had very little self-esteem. After all, I still was a teenager, and I was married and a bit overwhelmed. I had to hold my own.

I am glad I found a husband at an early age and got my aunts off my back. I was always told nobody would want to marry me. So, I married the first man I felt in love with, just to prove them wrong. They wanted me to improve my looks, my posture and the way I walked. My husband thought I was beautiful and that was all it mattered.

All said and done, I guess I turned out o.k. I guess my family pushed me in the right direction after all.

I remember, when I was a young teenager, walking to Church one Sunday morning. My uncle was following me, maybe 30 steps behind, I had not noticed him. When I returned home from church he stopped by our apartment and told me that I walked like a duck and need to change my walk. "Das ist nicht schoen", he said. (Your walk is not nice) The following Sunday I paid lots of attention to my walking skills.

I soon outgrew my awkwardness and teenage appearance. Being married helped me get more confidence, my husband approved of me, that's all what mattered. I was blond and by than had a bad haircut from a bad hairdresser in Georgia. Something else they did not know in Georgia, color or cut hair. Needless to say Georgia was the end of the world for me. My attitude contributed to my feelings. Of course it did not help that I was so homesick. The only thing we could do is go to the drive-in movie theater and eat hamburgers. I had no girlfriends, no female company, no mother to cuddle up with, no aunts to criticize me. There were other young new brides living on base at Ft. Benning, but we lived too far away to associate with them, approximately 10 miles one way. I was totally dependent on my husband. I did get my driver's license but we had only one car. No transportation, no bike, just a lonely house, the record player and me.

We drove to Atlanta to the beautiful Fox movie theater to see "Gone with the Wind". We toured the city before the movie and visited some sights where the movie was filmed.

"South Pacific" we also enjoyed at the Fox Movie Theater. It was lovely to get out occasionally and see a bit of the country side and how other people live.

When I left Germany my mother made sure I had a proper dowry with all the necessary household items, (the US Military shipped all my belonging for free) including china for twelve, my wedding silver which was a wedding gift from my grandmother. 12 towels, 12 sheets, sheets which did not fit the American size mattress. We received a toaster as a wedding present which was wired for 110, the European electric current.

I was also outfitted with the appropriate wardrobe including a pink/rose colored silk dress for more elegant functions/occasions, a Bolero topped it off. There was a lovely green and white gingham linen dress with full skirt and wide shoulder straps, and a black bare shoulder dress for dances. All made by our seamstress. (Not Tante Marga, she was too busy at that time with well paying customers). The silk dress I got to wear only once, the day I received my American citizenship. Due to my husband being in the military, I was able to become a US citizen within two years. The certificate reads I weigh 100 lbs. and I am 5'2 in height. At that time I did not realize what it meant giving up my German citizenship. Dual citizenship was not offered during that time. All I wanted was to go back to Germany, the sooner the better.

Spring of 1959 I got pregnant. I think that saved me from going crazy. I had something to look forward to, to occupy my mind. Doug was also very happy about the news. One of my husband's friends was kind enough to convert the currency of my electric sawing machine from 110volts to 220. I was able to make all my maternity clothes myself and besides a few shorts did not have to buy much. In those days we wore tops (I think they were called smog's) and skirts and I had fun preparing for the big event. I could sew without a pattern, something I learned from Tante Marga.

I had no idea how to take care of an infant, never learned anything about it. I had never been around babies, nobody had babies when I grew up. The population in Germany went down dramatically during the war years and many years thereafter. Thinking back, I was not ready for marriage and/or having babies. However, as I said before, I was a quick learner. Show me once and I got it.

The pregnancy was fairly uneventful except for the summer heat in Georgia. Every morning I got up at five o'clock to get my house work done, pressed my husband's uniforms and do the ironing. I ironed all our laundry, including underwear, dish towels and sheets. It kept me occupied for several hours. By 8 o'clock it got too hot and I had to lay down and rest. The Georgia heat is really brutal and was taking a toll on me. I never experienced hot sun like the Georgia sun before; just walking to the mail box was an effort but necessary; always looking for a letter from my parents. I wrote many letters to my parents, hundreds of letters, at least one every week, sometimes two. They answered each letter, even my father wrote to me.

I was so home sick. I felt so alone. No relatives, no friends and a husband who was gone a lot. In the month of December, my 8th month of pregnancy, I gained some extra pounds; Mutti had sent me a Christmas packet with lots of goodies. The doctor made me lose the extra six pounds in one week. He threatened to put me in hospital and promised a diet of spinach and grapefruit. The week after Christmas I had lost the six extra pounds and was right on target with my weight, not gaining more than 20 lbs. during the pregnancy. Unheard of today, but the doctor insisted and told me it was easier to deliver carrying the proper weight.

On January 15th early in the morning I went into labor.

My husband drove me to the hospital in Ft. Benning, GA and dropped me off at the maternity ward. The doctor said "good bye, soldier" we will call you when we have a baby. Again, I was alone. I was in Labor only four hours before I delivered a healthy baby boy. We called him Derek Martin. At that time, the medical profession was totally against mothers nursing their babies and all the new mothers were given a small pill every day to dry up their milk. Two days in hospital and $7.50 later, I was sent home with a newborn and no help.

One of my husband's friend's wife (an experienced mother) came over and showed me how to bath my infant. There were no classes available on how to take care of a baby and I cannot remember why I not even had a book on the subject. Doug was able to get three days off to help. He was in charge of making the baby's formula every day and he did a great job. I never heard of formula before or paid any attention to the subject. Where I came from babies were nursed.

We purchased a washing machine but could not afford a dryer. I developed allergies with major sneezing attacks. Clothes lines were put up between the pine trees in the back yard to dry the dozens of cloths diapers, baby clothes and the rest of our laundry. I stuffed cotton up my nose to stop the drip, drip, drip.

The hot summers in Georgia were exhausting. But how could I complain when my husband had to play in military parades in the marching band under the boiling sun. That was punishment. Of course our house was not air conditioned, we could not even effort to buy a fan.

My mother-in-law sent us a small baby crib, one which had been passed down from generation to generation. My baby got heat rash, so every evening we went for a drive in the car and/or to a drive-in movie to cool off and escape the heat. Our house did not cool down till after midnight, probably no insulation at all.

On those rides in the country site, I noticed many shacks and little houses, some hiding under trees, others just surrounded by bushes. They were mostly occupied by black people, exposed to the Georgian sun with little or no shade. If they could do it, I can do it.

Make the best of a situation, I could do it.

Doug came home with the most exciting news. He managed to get a transfer back to Germany. I jumped for joy. He was to join the 8th Infantry Division Band in Bad Kreuznach, Germany. We are to leave Georgia in October.

Derek was a sweet little boy, the joy and love of our lives, he kept me totally busy. Besides a summer heat rash from the hot Georgian summer sun, he was healthy and a pleasure to have around. At the end of summer we sold our house, payed off all of our debts with proceeds from the house sale, and drove up north.

Before we left for Germany on our overseas tour, we visit my in-laws and introduce Gertrude and Frank to their new grandson. Derek was dressed in a beautiful little red coat and looked adorable. He was a big hit. We stayed one week and Doug showed me the Finger Lakes Region which was very colorful that time of year. I also met some of his High school friends.

It was autumn in NY, and early one morning in October we said good bye and drove to NY City in our brand new light blue Dodge

Sedan. We boarded the USS Patch to Bremerhaven, Germany. The almost one week long trip was exciting, all American soldiers and families on board. Lots of folks got sea sick, the three of us fared well. Derek loved being on the ocean liner, (nothing luxurious), but it was entertaining. We had a private room with two bunk beds and a crib. Three nice meals per day were served, Derek kept eating and I had to order double portions for him. The fresh air made him hungry. Several times it got stormy, the crib had to be tied to our bunk beds; the hatches were closed, the dining room tables were secured before the dishes could crash.

From Bremerhaven we took the train to Wuerzburg. Oh, what a happy reunion! My parents met us at the train station with flowers and gifts and I handed over my baby. Derek met his grandparents, he had a complete family now. They welcomed him with open arms, I felt like re-born. Just like my name, Renate (that's what it means in Latin, re-born). The smell of the air early in the morning at the train station in Wuerzburg, including pollution, let me forget the past two years. All was good again, I was re-born.

Bad Kreuznach

(Bad meaning Spa)

1960-1963

Doug had a few vacation days left, which he was able to spend in Wuerzburg before he had to report to Bad Kreuznach to assume his military duties. He also had to search for an apartment for us. That turned out to be somewhat of a difficult task. We were put on a waiting list and needed to find interim housing. A small, fully furnished small garden cottage became available for rent. It was converted from a chicken coop to a well decorated tiny cottage with a make-shift kitchen, shower and bath. It served us as temporary housing until military housing was available. Not too bad for a former chicken coop. Derek stayed with my parents. The German people leased out every room they owned and could spare, all for the almighty dollar.

I got pregnant either on the boat or in the chicken coop.

In Bad Kreuznach

In August 1961, just after we got settled in our new apartment I delivered my second baby, another little boy. We gave him his father's name since I only had picked out names for a girl. Douglas Stephen. He weighed in at 8 lbs., a beautiful and healthy baby with blond curly hair.

My parents were more than happy to help out and stayed with us as long as needed. They helped taking care of my two babies, new born Dougie and 18 months old Derek, who by that time knew more of the German language than English. By age two Derek was bi-lingual.

Soon after we got settled in Bad Kreuznach, Germany, my husband put together a jazz band to work the Officer's and NCO

Clubs in our area. He was very busy but as always, we needed extra money.

The problem was, to get hired in the Clubs, the band had to have a female singer.

Soldiers wanted to look at a pretty female. Well, that was a big problem. The band did not have a singer. The only requirement to get hired was – carry a tune and look good, not necessary in that order. The band members were unsuccessful finding that missing link, a female singer.

Last resort, they turned to me. I was the chosen one out of necessity and extra money sounded good to me having a growing family. I had a pretty good, untrained voice, a very good ear and natural rhythm, but never performed in public. Well, wasn't that what I always wanted, sing and perform on stage?

Opportunity knocking at my door, I learned to sing. My husband handed me a microphone and we started rehearsing. "Bye, Bye Birdie, My Funny Valentine, Basin Street, Stormy Weather", just to mention a few. I had quite a selection, at least 20 tunes were needed to get me through four hours of entertaining. Soon I found out it was not easy to sing in a foreign language and express feelings, I had to learn the lyrics word for word, memorize every word and did not know what I was singing about. Well, maybe not quite that bad.

A new wardrobe was also necessary and a reliable babysitter. I went back to Wuerzburg to my old seamstress and she produces several beautiful and attractive cocktail dresses and I was on my way. I must have done all right, the band got hired and we signed a contract playing three nights a week in the Officers Club.

Renata's music poster

There was a German band based out of Mainz, close to Frankfurt, who also worked the American club circuit. They had the same problem, "female singer" needed. Pretty soon I had an offer to sing with that German band. I sang for both bands three nights a week in different clubs. I worked Baumholder and Bad Kreuznach, sometimes as far away as Landstuhl. The long drive home in the middle of the night really was the problem. We carpooled and since I had the largest vehicle, several of the band members enjoyed to be transported in the larger American car. I was the chauffeur for half the group. I loved it but it was not manageable. I just could not survive on four to five hours of sleep most nights. My babies demanded my time.

However there were advantages working with the German group, they paid me more money and the band usually had three horn players.

Several times I was able to tour Germany on short vacations or music engagements. I was invited to go along on some band trips, my parents always willing to stay with the boys. Doug traveled a lot with the 8th Division Band, he had the good fortune to play for President Kennedy when the President visited Berlin.

He heard the President's speech: "Ich bin ein Berliner" in person.

Before too long I found myself pregnant again. How could this happen? Number three on the way. Someone told me later the number three baby is always an unexpected surprise and I experience that. I sang with the band thru my sixth month before anyone noticed. The fashionable clothing style that year were "Sack" dresses and it was perfect for me. Design straight down, like a sack.

I felt good. In my ninth month I found out I had the RH factor and the doctors had me all shook up. Several doctors were in the delivery room with me, including an incubator and a helicopter was standing by to transfer my baby to a larger hospital. Stuart Theodor was born in March 1963 and he was a healthy baby with a big dimple in his chin. The nurse said he looked just like Kirk Douglas. So cute, only 6lbs.8 ozs.

Shortly after Stuart's birth, Doug got orders to return to the US in October. We were not ready for this but knew from the beginning of our three year tour.

Another difficult good bye for all of us, especially my parents. They welcomed these grand babies into their lives and now I take them away. I had a tough and difficult time also leaving my parents and relatives again, but I had my own family now and I belonged to them. What a heartbreak for all.

"You make your bed and you lay in it", it's a German saying and one of the many my Mutti kept reminding me of.

These three years flew bye so quickly, we were happy growing our family. Making babies had to stop so, I did not want to have a football team, a musical trio was just fine.

Keep Singing

The five of us, three year old Derek, Dougie two years old and Stuart six months, departed Germany in October 1963 by military plane from Frankfurt to Ft. Dix, NJ. We checked into a hotel room at the army base.

Our vehicle was shipped at an earlier date and had arrived in the USA several days before we did. The next day after our arrival from Germany, Doug had to leave early in the morning to retrieve our car at some port in New York City and I was left alone for a whole day with my three babies. We had to manage three meals in the cafeteria. One kid was climbing out of a high chair while the other was climbing on a chair. Cafeterias and I just don't seem to get along. To this day I do not like to eat in a cafeteria, if I can possibly help it. When I see young mothers today, struggling with their babies, all I can say is: "Been there, done that". Not recommendable having three babies in three years, especially when there is no help available. A nightmare, I never was so happy to see my husband.

Our new destination was Hampton, VA. Finding housing at an Army base is always difficult and the only thing available was a summer cottage on the beach. O.K. for a short while, maybe till the end of November it could be manageable. It will be fun living on the beach. However, it was already the end of October and we knew winter was approaching. We could not stay during the winter month, so we kept on looking for more appropriate housing. "Let's settle in for a while," Doug said. Our furniture had not arrived yet, so the furnished cottage will be fine for a few weeks.

We kept looking for something more permanent.

I was walking with my kiddies on the beach, baby Stuart in a stroller. Derek and Dougie enjoying the sand on the beach. A neighbor lady came running out of her house, screaming "President Kennedy was shot, he is dead". The date was 11/22/1963. I hurried my children back to the cottage, sat down on the couch and cried. I held my babies tight. How could this happen, are we at war? WAR is a bad word for me. Were we attacked by another country? No information was available to me at this time, I did not have a radio to listen too. Of course we did not have a television either, since we just arrived back in the States and we were not going to buy one till we could occupy more permanent quarters. When my husband came home from base we went straight to Sears Roebuck's department store to purchase a television set. The next three days we spent watching the screen. Everybody was glued to the TV. You could not find any people on the street. People were in shock and seriously grieving. Murdering the president put the country and the world in deep mourning.

Doug had to make the big decision to either re-enlist in the military or leave the service. The Vietnam War was getting lots of attention and it was inevitable, by re-enlisting, Doug would be shipped off to Vietnam on his next assignment. I was very upset and told him I will not be in a strange country with three small children, knowing my husband is fighting a war on another continent. I was not going to move to Upstate NY either, to move in and live with my in-laws. Doug's mother wrote a letter to encourage her son to get a discharge from the military and return to NY.

The decision was made to leave the Army after 12 years of active duty. Doug had the opportunity to join the Army reserve to finish his 20 years military service. Of course he had to find a job to support our family. I was brought up with the idea, the husband gets a job and supports his family, wife stays home with the children. Old customs are hard to break. By this time I also become a bit tired of moving the family, especially since I had to do most of the work.

It was a difficult decision and again I felt uprooted. No job, no home, feeling like a Gypsy. I use the word Gypsy, it's like a Nomad, a person who keeps wandering. I wanted to settle down, preferably in a house of our own.

We stayed another month in Hampton, VA after Doug's discharge from the military. He was offered a great steady gig in a Country Club playing the piano, cocktail music from 5-9p.m. The tip jar was over flowing every night and he made a good living at the Club working three hours a day. It was not what I had dreamed of for our future, but I enjoyed having my husband home all day and spending the day with the family. However, for the more secure and better future of our sons we decided to move back to Doug's family and start settling down.

I also did not want to deny my kids a life without grandparents and miss the sense of family security. With $500 in our pocket, three little boys in tow and all our worldly possessions in a small trailer hooked on to our vehicle, we headed up north to New York State, the Finger Lakes region in Canandaigua to live with my in-laws for a short while. This arrangement lasted six weeks, longer than I expected, I have to admit. Doug soon found a job at Gleason's, a manufacturing plant in Rochester, hopefully to soon get a better job at the world renowned famous Eastman Kodak Company. They employed about 40,000 men and women in the Rochester area. I was told, once you work for Kodak, you will always have a good job. The job with Eastman Kodak did not materialize, Doug was not hired.

Just as well - we all know better today. Kodak filed Chapter 11 bankruptcy in January of 2012. The end of an era for Rochester, NY.

After six weeks living in the same house with my in-laws, we purchased a brand new three bedroom trailer, 12' x 60' all furnished and it was sparkly clean. My in-laws had several dogs and many cats and that was not my cup of tea. Before we purchase the "Mobil Home", we looked at apartments and houses to rent. Everything that we could afford was of dark interior and dark dingy wood and small windows. Houses were not kept up, they were all in desperate need of repair. Not the style I could be happy in. Canandaigua was a sleepy little town, no updates had been made to any houses or buildings. Newcomers were not readily accepted into the community, the town was at a standstill. That was 1964.

I liked the lake and the hills and the scenery which reminded me a lot of Germany. It did not take too long to get used to the pretty landscape.

Derek, Doug and Stuart on Grandma's farm

Our brand new trailer was fully furnished and was quickly delivered to a small park on Lake Shore Drive. It was quite handy that a laundry-mat was within walking distance. We needed to be by ourselves and raise our children. We also needed money. The financial security, including health insurance while in the military, was gone. One time, I went to a dentist and walked out of the office without paying. I had to adjust to civilian life. No more freebies, like in the military, or living under my father's roof.

Doug took the civil service exam to apply for a job at the US Post Office, a good secure job where his military time counted towards his retirement. It took about six months to get the desired employment. He also had joined the National Guard.

In the meantime he used his musical talents and played dance music. He played piano for dances, weddings, bar mitzvah etc. Soon he put together his own trio, sometimes he added a horn player and they played as a quartet. Jobs came from as far away as Ithaca and any place in the Finger Lakes region. He was offered to play two nights a week at a nightclub in Ithaca, called "Box Car" a well-known night spot owned by a popular TV personality. I believe his son was managing the club.

Again, for that particular job a female singer was requested and soon I started to go with the band. I could deal with this only for a short time, again I ran out of energy. My place was at home with my children, but I also needed a life and more money. I decided to look for other a job, there must be employment for me somewhere. It was very necessary for me to become my own person, get to know some people. Contribute to society might be the better word. I still had not made any friends or did know a person besides my family and the in-laws. It was very lonely, I did not have one local friend.

It was not an easy time for me to adjust to Canandaigua, I knew nobody. I misses all the friends and relatives I had in Germany. My mother-in-law had introduced me to some older ladies, took me to the "Home-Bureau". But these ladies were all much older than I. I was not ready to join a senior citizens group.

Soon we joined St. John's Episcopal Church and I took my boys to Sunday school. I did not know how "Sunday school" worked, we did not have that in Germany. I was taught religion in school. However I felt, some religion could not hurt my children, they will also have the opportunity to make new friends.

Instead of myself attending church service, I dropped the boys off at church and went back home to do my ironing. Then I drove back to Church to pick them up. I should have gone to Church myself but I felt very awkward and uncomfortable with strangers. They were very friendly towards each other but not towards me. Again I felt like the outsider not fitting in. People were very cliquish in church. One of the first things they ask me "where are you from and where did you go to collage"? Well, that makes good sense but immediately it made me feel like an outsider.

Soon I found the right answer, I told them "I was born and educated in Europe". That took care of their questions, most of them did not know anything about Europe. I learned to hold my own.

I did not fit in with these people, they certainly did not welcome me in this small town. Canandaigua was very cliquish in the early 60's.

Just about all men and women were smoking, including my husband. Women did not have pride in their appearance (they walked on Main Street with curlers in their hair) and I notices they were not good housekeepers either. I guess I complained just about everything, nothing was right. The thing was, I was homesick again. I wrote my Mutti about my misery. She immediately booked a trip to cross the ocean on the boat called the "Bremen". She was here within a few weeks and moved into the trailer with us. She stayed for a months and all was well.

When my husband and I first started dating, he offered me a cigarette. I remember it well. I started coughing so badly and embarrassed myself to the point that people stared at me. That was the only puff I ever took. What a good life saving decision that turned out to be.

Having only secretarial training in Germany did not help much in pursuing a job in this country. I did some translating and also tutored some high school students with their German studies from our neighborhood. However that did not improve my employment opportunities in the USA. My choices were very limited.

All I had was a good personality (I thought) and a will to work to better myself. I enjoyed studying people, I always had an opinion. Soon I figured out that I could do most anything, but I also knew I did not want to sit behind a desk, like I did in my very first job. I just needed to figure out the American customs, personalities and lifestyle and where I do fit in.

I read an advertisement in the paper, "Waitress wanted". I put on my best outfit, a light blue, very elegant custom made and perfectly fitting suit (Jackie Kennedy style) high heels and off I went. I looked like I had an interview for an executive position. Always put your best foot forward, my Mutti taught me. The restaurant, a very popular Italian style eating establishment on Lake Shore Drive was just down the street from where we lived in our trailer park. Several middle-aged men, plus one older gentleman (the patriarch) were present when I entered the well-known family-style restaurant.

My heart was pounding.

"I am applying for the job as a waitress", I said. One of the men, his name was John asked my name and as soon as I opened my mouth he detected my accent." Can you start at 5:00 o'clock"? "Yes, I certainly can". You are hired. We will see you than. The two other brothers and the patriarch, their father, knotted their heads, approving the decision. They gave me a thorough look from head to toe and walked back into what turned out to be the kitchen.

On my way home I stopped at the local Woolworth store and purchase a white uniform dress and white shoes. When Doug came home I informed him of my decision that I accepted a job as a waitress and he will have to spend more time with our sons caring for them. For a few hours on the weekends we hired a baby sitter. Some things needed to be arranged or changed, I needed transportation was a biggie.

My father in-law had an old station wagon which was dropped off and abandoned on their farm behind the barn. He had purchased a newer vehicle when he retired. This station wagon was not road worthy, rust was taking over. He agreed to let us have the car for free. It did not cost very much to get a license, registration and a few repairs needed to be done. I was happy to drive the old jalopy back and forth to work. After a short while Doug felt sorry for me driving this old rust bucket and soon agreed to let me drive our new maroon colored Dodge sedan. By then, Doug was working at the Post office on Main Street, just a short driving distance from the Mobil Home Park to North Main Street. His musical instruments fitted easier in the station wagon, so it was a fair trade.

We got a swing set for the boys and a little plastic pool for them to splash around in and cool off. They also enjoyed playing on my very clean floors inside the trailer. I took walks with them, little Stuart in the stroller. We explored the neighborhood, walked to the lake and found Roseland Park Amusement park. The kids enjoyed the music from the carousel and the smell of food from the vendors. What fun and so close to where we lived, a five minute walk.

Every day at four o'clock I started getting ready for my waitress job. Stuart was only a little over one year old, he threw himself on the floor outside the bathroom door and screamed his head off. He did not want me to go. It broke my heart every day. Little Dougie and Derek were fine spending more time with their Dad or a baby sitter.

I learned the work routine at the restaurant very quickly under the watchful eye of John, one of the owners. Soon I became one of their most reliable and dependable waitresses. German punctuality and accuracy was valued by the Italian owners. I was a trust-worthy employee. What was even better, I was from the "old country".

I became aware that I really enjoyed being around people and it helped my personality and people skills.

People enjoyed interacting and communicating with me. I became a "people person" and soon realized I never would have been happy in an office job just working behind a desk - I needed people. I never had waited on tables before and soon learned it was hard work. However, it was enjoyable for me to meet and talk to different people and I did make good money.

This was 1964/65, a fish fry at the restaurant cost 85 cents, a cup of coffee was a nickel. Business was good, Friday evening's customers stood in line for an available table.

During the first year working at the restaurant I saved enough money so we could purchase a building lot. One acre of land for $1,000. It was on Coy Rd. west side of the lake, about ten miles south of the City of Canandaigua. No public water or sewer available, so we dug a well and put in a septic system. We did have a gorgeous view of the lake and grapevines, adjoining our property.

My husband hired a contractor to start building our new home. This man was already retired from his carpenter job, but needed to substitute his income and occupy his free time. He did not have any family and enjoyed getting back to work. Doug became his assistant and "go-for". The two worked well together and the house situated on the one acre parcel with lake view turned out well. 1966/67 we sold our trailer and we moved into our new home.

I did well as a waitress on Lake Shore Drive. The second year working after we moved into the new house, I purchased my first new car. A small Pinto $2,900, all paid for in cash. I was able to save my tips, Doug's income paid for our living expenses. I had my financial independence back. I knew I could do it.

As soon as our house was completed, my parents came that

summer and every summer thereafter to visit. It was necessary for them to stay in close contact with their grandsons. Of course I loved to see my parents also when they came to visit. We showed them NY State, Niagara Falls, the Thousand Islands and Toronto, Cape Cod and Boston in Massachusetts. All the popular sights were on the list. Over the next 20 years they probably made 15- to 20 trips to the USA.

During one of her visits here, my mother broke her arm. She was walking our German Shepard dog, Fritz Friedrich on a leash, when he tried to pull away from her. Mutti went down. Fritz was quite a handful, a strong dog. Mutti ended up with a cast on her arm and she acted like she was the first person ever who broke an arm. My father had to come immediately from Germany since she needed someone's full attention and take care of her. Yes, she always was spoiled by my father.

To award her for her bravery, we made a vacation trip to Plymouth Rock. We stayed in a lovely hotel and my parents had an especially beautiful hotel room with a great view of the Atlantic Ocean. Mutti did not want to leave the room, she settled in and stated it was too expensive and beautiful, so she had to spent every minute in the room and not leave it. She had to make full use of the extravagant accommodations.

The house on Coy Rd. served us well. To my dismay a lot of time was spent on the road driving back and forth to Canandaigua. Sadly, there were hardly any children in close proximity for the boys to play with, and I had to take them to town for activities. They took music lessons, were involved in boy scouts, church, skiing, you name it, we tried to do it all. It was mostly me who did the driving back and forth to town. Doug had to work all week including every Saturday at the Post Office, on weekends he played music. Sunday he deserved some rest and it was also family time. I got tired driving the 10 miles (one way) back and forth to Canandaigua for the boy's activities, sometimes three times a day. It was especially hard in the winter with blowing snow and icy roads.

Working at the restaurant offered me the opportunity to meet people and communicate with other folks with likewise interests. Soon I made the acquaintance of a German couple. Art and Rita, they became our good and trusted friends. They had emigrated from Germany and settled here in Canandaigua, just like we did. Sometimes I think they were my life savers. We had things in common and could talk about cooking, the old country, the time during and after the war and life in general. They shared their war experiences with us, different than mine; Art was born in Ukraine and had to leave his homeland, flee from the Russians. He had spent a few years in Germany before immigrating to the USA.

Rita was an excellent chef and an especially great baker. I got to enjoy some wonderful home cooked German meals. They had four children, the two younger ones being born in the USA. Unfortunately their oldest son Willie, was killed in the Viet Nam war at age 20. What a tragedy, he was a German citizen.

Doug did not miss social life as much as I did, he had his job and his music which made him happy.

Several years later we met another couple, Don and Ursula. Ursula was from Kaiserslautern, Germany and had married an American soldier stationed in Germany the same I had.

The six of us became the best friends and we stayed that way for the remainder of our lives. Ursel and I are the only ones left from the group.

The decision was made to sell the house on Coy Road.

We sold the house in 1972 and built a modest home in the city.

It was a Cape Cod style, four bedrooms, two baths, finished off basement for the kids to play in.

I took the boys to the "Old swim school" at Kershaw Park, they loved learning how to swim and play in the park. I met ladies my own age with their children. The boys and I made new friends. As they got a little older, they enjoyed riding their bicycles to the lake by themselves, they walked to school by themselves with friends from the neighborhood.

The realtor who sold our house on Coy Rd., Ron Schaeffer, also a musician friend of my husband, suggested for me to get my Real Estate license. He said I have the right personality for the job. I thought about it for a while and soon Doug and I agreed this would be a good opportunity for me to start a new career.

We also got more involved in community activities, joined the church choir at St. John's Episcopal Church were we remained active members of the choir for 25 years.

I traveled to Germany almost every fall to see my parents.

In 1972 we took a family vacation to Germany. The time was perfect for my sons to re-connect with family, meet the cousins and learn about my homeland. Helga and Helmut had two daughters by then and the boys got well acquainted with their cousins and the rest of their family. They got spoiled by all. We stayed a full month and enjoyed every moment. So many wonderful memories!

After nine years working as a waitress, I quit my job and said good bye to the seasonal restaurant. It was good while it lasted and I learned a lot. I learned how to deal with people.

My next business opportunity, I became a Real Estate Agent.

I studied, took my test and soon received my NY State Real Estate license. I became a licensed Real Estate Agent. "AL-Co Properties" asked me to join the company and Don McWilliams taught me most everything I needed to know. It was a small office in Canandaigua and perfect for me to learn the ropes. The flexible work schedule, meeting and talking to people, showing houses, all a plus and every so often I even got a paycheck. After two years in business I took the Brokers exam, became a Real Estate Broker and moved on working for "Roc Vitalone Realty", a larger firm located on Main Street in Canandaigua. I loved my new found career, working with people and assisting them finding a home. I worked with Roc V. for nine years. At that time I was asked to join "Coldwell Banker" which after several years became "Griffith Realty".

The Piano

My husband inherited "the Piano", a lovely baby grand from his Aunt Mini, who was Doug's great aunt.

Mini was an old spinster, a talented Artist who painted water colors, mostly still life's. She also did exquisite needle work. (I still have a dozen gorgeous dinner napkins designed and hand crocket by her). Amongst one of her talents, she was also an accomplished pianist. She started to teach her nephew, than six year old Douglas, how to play the piano. It was a serious business for her, young Douglas showed lots of talent and soon he became Aunt Mini's musical prodigy. Mini supported her frugal lifestyle with piano lessons and painting water colors and oil paintings. Douglas was groomed and trained and expected to become a concert pianist. The lessons where very important and each and every day he had to practice his lessons for two hours after he came home from school. Mother Gertrude was in total agreement with Aunt Mini and between the two they made sure practicing the piano was his main job and entertainment. He followed the rules for many years. He was an only child and little King Tot.

In his teenage years Doug began to rebel this regimen and put a sudden stop to the piano lessons and practice. His mother and Aunt Mini were in awe.

Shortly after his High school graduation Doug enlisted in the

Military. After basic training and several years of service in the military, he was fortunate enough to join the Army band. He played the piano in the band and along the way he studied to play several other instruments, like the clarinet, drums and other keyboard instuments. He was able to play snare drums in the marching band, other instruments in the orchestra and band. He discovered his love for Jazz and soon started playing in nightclubs, NCO and officers clubs. The Military band was shipped to Wuerzburg, Germany in 1955 for a three year tour.

Doug was slim and tall, 6'2" with dark blond curly hair. He was handsome and polite and paid lots of attention to me. I was smitten.

This guy could play the piano, I loved it. He played songs for me, like "My Funny Valentine", "Cry me a river", the blues and all the beautiful Ballads. I instantly I fell in love with Jazz, the piano and him. I could listen to him playing the piano for hours.

I always wanted a piano but we did not have room or money for big purchases and I had to settle for an accordion.

Back to the piano. Aunt Mini willed Doug her baby grand piano after her death.

After Doug's father had retired from Graflex in Rochester, Gertrude and Frank moved from their home in Rochester to Canandaigua. They had purchased 33 acres of land with an old 1800 style farmhouse, which was in desperate need of repair and updating. There also was a two-story barn and several smaller outbuildings. Big project. The piano was moved from Aunt Mini's house in Rochester and delivered to the old farmhouse to find temporary housing till Doug had his own home and could accommodate the piano.

The baby grand was dark walnut in color and soon a place was found in one of the multiple parlors. Before long, the piano was covered with every magazine Gertrude had subscribed too.

The Reber's became gentlemen/farmers. They planted grape vines, six acres of vineyard. There were blue Concord grapes, white Niagara and pink Catawba grapes. All delicious and most were used for juice. Some of the grapes were taken to the Grape festival in Naples, the rest were sold to Widmer's winery also in Naples.

Barn animals were added, like two cows, two pigs and many smaller animals including chickens and a rooster. They owned at least three dogs at a time and cats multiplied fast. Gertrude loved all animals.

Frank and Gertrude also had huge gardens with more vegetables and fruit than what they could handle. Very little money was left over to restore the house. The house was not on the list of priorities, the animals were. Dogs and cats multiplied.

When I arrived in 1958 they just had installed indoor plumbing, however the outhouse was still in use. The remodeling job was done to impress me and so was the indoor plumbing!

Doug enjoyed playing the piano for me on our very few visits at his parents' home. This piano is mine, he announced to me on one of our trips home. When we have our own home, we will move the piano there.

Well, after 12 years in the military, we decided to join civilian life. Doug left the military and we ended up in Canandaigua. I like to say "we" got discharged because I always felt I was in the service with him. I spit-shined his boots, shined the brass buckles, ironed his shirts and had three babies. I was part of the team. In 1964 we moved to Canandaigua, lived for six weeks in his parent's home, than purchased a brand new mobile home. We left the military with $500, exactly the amount we needed for a down payment on our new fully furnished trailer. It was transported to a small Mobil Home Park, situated at the outskirts of town.

Of course the piano did not fit and had to remain in the old Farmhouse. After two years living in the small trailer park in Canandaigua, we had saved up enough money to build a new home in the country, about 10 miles south of Canandaigua, the last house in the Canandaigua school district. It was important to us that the children would start in the proper school district and graduate from the same school.

It was a contemporary style home, redwood siding, 1800 square foot split level with enough room in a corner of the living room to accommodate the piano. Our lake view on top of a hill was breathtaking with several acres of grapevines between the lake and the house. We could not afford Lakefront property, but a view was the next best thing.

Oh, the piano has a good place here with us on the farm, said Gertrude. It costs too much money to move, it will take special movers and you will miss the space in your home. Let's move it later!!!!! It has a lovely spot here, it fits perfect.

We lived on Coye Rd. for five years. We enjoyed living in the country but it was just too inconvenient to live so far from playmates, school and activities. Sometimes I drove back and forth to town two and three times a day, 10 miles each way. I had enough of that. My husband was busy with his job at the Post office, playing music three nights every week and all the running around including transporting the boys, was left up to me.

We decided to sell the house. We built a new home in the City of Canandaigua on Douglas Drive. 1800 square feet, four bedrooms, two baths, Cape Cod style home. It served us well. The boys could ride their bicycles all over town and to the lake. I soon found out there was no room for the piano. The thought came to mind, "will we ever have the piano in our home"?

Doug continued his music business on a portable electric "Hohner" keyboard instrument, which he could move fairly easy from dance job to dance job. He played steady at the beautiful historic "Lafayette Inn" in Geneva, the Country Clubs in and around the area, Dance Clubs, weddings and bar mitzvahs'. The "Doug Reber Trio" became well known and was a popular and desired musical group for all occasions. It was good extra income for us besides him working at the local post office with many benefits. All his military time counted towards retirement and he ended up finishing 25 years in the Army reserve unit in Rochester.

In 1982 my mother-in-law passed away shortly after my father-in-law's death. My husband being the only child had the responsibility taking care of the estate and that meant emptying out a 2400 square feet house, a two story barn and a berry drying house with three generations of collectables, old stuff and old furniture, so called antiques and more "stuff".

Well, here was my last chance. I called the movers, pushed some furniture aside in my son's bedroom and had the piano delivered to our relatively small house on Douglas Drive, that was definitely not built to accommodate a baby grand piano. It was not convenient either, the piano took up half of my son's bedroom and he was not a happy camper. It was not even pretty to look at, what was I thinking? I covered it with a large black table clothes/shawl with long fringes, also an antique from the Reber/Jones' family estate.

My mother-in-law was a Jones, granddaughter of W. Martin Jones, a lawyer and secretary to William Henry Seward. A lot of history came with the family.

I decided we needed a bigger house and soon I had Doug convinced that was the way to go. We have been living on Douglas Drive for 12 years, the boys were ready to move out of the house after graduating from High School. I was well established in the Real Estate business and could count on good repeat business.

I had found a suitable building site on West Lake Road about one mile south of Main Street. Easy commute for all my travels. Soon we started construction on building our dream home. Young people would call it now their "for-ever home". We had a basic plan but Doug and I made all the necessary changes to turn it into my dream home. A living room 26'x28' with enough space to accommodate the baby grand piano was on top of my list. Finally it would have the proper space, a new home where it could be admired and displayed. Taking a closer look at the piano, I realized that it was not a show stopper at all, nothing to show off. It had dark and dirty walnut wood and did not match any of my selected pieces of furniture, a mixture of contemporary and antique.

I had the whole piano dismantled, the wood stripped, strings and keys replaced and/or repaired and it had to be tuned several times to hold a note. After four months of repair and restoration, it was ready for our home and spacious living room. Finally it was a show piece, much lighter in color than the original color. It was placed in a perfect corner in our bright and airy living room. It was polished and cared for by me and played beautifully by my husband for the next 12, short, years.

We hosted many wonderful parties with Doug playing the piano. We both enjoyed cooking, Doug being the better chef. However, my German cuisine was always well received.

Doug died of esophageal cancer after fighting cancer for three years. He was 62 years old. The piano turned silent.

Only three month before his death we were blessed with a beautiful granddaughter. Doug willed the piano to our new granddaughter Sydney. I kept polishing and cherishing "my" piano. My son and his wife had no space in their modest home to accommodate the baby grand.

It will cost too much to move the piano and it fits here perfectly.…. I heard those words before. This time those words were spoken by me. I just wanted to hang on to the memories, the history and of course my husband playing that piano.

My Family Is Growing

Stuart had married pretty Seana Rodney Sept. 3rd 1988. It was a beautiful wedding. We had guests for their wedding arriving from Germany. My cousin Helga with husband Helmut, their two adult daughters plus my mother, in tow.

They flew into Toronto International Airport in Canada and I was excited to pick them up. Doug and I only owned two five passenger cars. I needed a car to accommodate five guests plus their luggage. A good friend of mine insisted I drive his Station wagon to Canada; I happily accepted his offer. It is a three plus hour trip and the traffic was horrendous. Long wait at the border crossing, the QEW in Canada, an extremely busy main highway. Trucks were passing me right and left and the thought crossed my mind, if I take my foot of the accelerator, I will be sausage. There were eighteen wheelers on each side of me, plus in front and back. Just keep driving, keep the foot on the gas, I told myself.

I was running short on time. At the airport I had a difficult time finding the exit to the parking garage, got stuck in the wrong traffic lane and circled the airport several times. By now I was really late to meet my company and that did not help my disposition. A German is never late, and I live by that rule. I got very frustrated, pulled the car over at a "10 minute parking spot only", locked the vehicle and ran inside the airport.

I figured by now they should have collected their luggage, gone thru customs and showing up by the exit door.

Wrong!

Several flights from Europa landed within the hour, all these folks had to clear customs and collect their many suit cases. There must have been over a thousand people in the same place and it took me a while to find my relatives. They needed two luggage cart to transport their suit cases to the gate. Just to mention, they were staying at my house for several weeks. I guess it never occurred to them that we own a washing machine and dryer.

It took more than two hours for them to clear customs. We finally made our exit from the airport terminal and started searching for the car. No car in sight, did I forget the area where I left the car? No, the car was gone, it was towed away. By then I was wishing to experience a stroke and die on the spot. I told my cousins, please take a seat on your suit cases and don't move. Strange, the police are always here when you don't want them but if you need them, where are they. I searched and finally found the airport police department in a lower level of the building and about a mile away from my location. I was informed the car was towed away by a private company to a secure location on the other side of Toronto.

I found myself a taxi cab for the 45 minute ride, paid $85 to get the car out of jail and drove back across the city of Toronto to the airport. I believe it took me about three hours for the journey. My guests were on the verge of exhaustion, some asleep and famished sitting on their suit cases. They looked like refugees. Not a good way to arrive in a foreign country with not enough English language skills to communicate.

We all piled in the car, suitcases on top of people. I was tired and hungry also but felt worse for my poor mother who had to tolerate such treatment at her age, 79 years old to be correct. It was night time, very dark and difficult to see. My passengers were asleep in no time since the time difference put them at about 3 a.m. the next day. The airport traffic was heavy as usual, but soon I was on the QEW and at the border. The border control was another problem since my mother had a new passport issued just before this trip and forgot to insert her visa. They wanted to detain her. My nerves were shot. I literally told the border patrol if they want to keep my mother, do so. Just keep her and let her sleep on a cot.

Well, after negotiations and the consideration of my mother's age, they let us enter the USA. Pile everybody in the car again, we headed to US RT I 90. After a short while I noticed no familiar road signs, it was so dark, I had enough trouble staying awake and seeing the road. I drove on I-90 west, the way to Erie, Pennsylvania. I took the wrong turn, west instead of east.

Well, we did get home that night. The next day I returned the car to its owner, unharmed, and I never told him the story of his vehicle.

We had a marvelous time with my German relatives here for the wedding. The wedding went off without problems and everybody was happy.

We showed the cousins the many beautiful Finger Lakes and the Up State New York region, the City of Rochester and of course Niagara Fall. We introduced them to some popular American cuisine, Hamburgers and/or Hot dogs and they especially enjoyed Chili Con Carne and American style Pizza. My cousin learned how to fix Chili and I had to send the Chili spices to Germany, at that time they could not purchase those products.

Our life became routine, the boys grew up. Derek chose to become a hair dresser, opening his own salon/business in 1994. Over the years he owned several different homes and enjoyed decorating them in different styles and décor.

Doug also liked working with his hands and become a contractor. within a few years he established his own business. He also loved skiing and soon decided to move to Park City, Utah, where he built beautiful homes in the mountains. In 2001 he returned home and married a lovely girl from Rochester, Lauren Russo; they divorced in 2013.

Stuart enjoyed working in the sales business after completing his education at Delhi. He became a Sales Manager for a Cadillac car dealership and by now has worked for the same company for more than 30 years. Their three off-springs are my beautiful grandchildren.

Picture of Stuart & Seana's wedding

My Three Boys

My German Bond Is Broken

After my father's death in 1983, Mutti remained in her apartment in Wuerzburg. She enjoyed life being close to her two sister, Emmi and Marga. They shared mealtimes together in different restaurants and enjoyed their "Golden Years" in Wuerzburg. My father had passed at age 75, heart issues.

After my father's passing, I made the trip across the pond at least twice each year to visit with my Mutti. Due to her almost lifelong illnesses and frailness, she had been pampered and very spoiled by my father. He did everything for her and I continued to do so. After he died, I flew to Germany to pack her suitcase so she could travel with me to the US. She refused to pack her own suitcase and unless I would do it for her, she just would not travel. So, I flew to Germany, packed her suitcase and we flew back together to the States.

The trip back to Germany was a little bit more difficult. Doug and I drove Mutti to Toronto airport so she could fly non-stop to Frankfurt. My cousin Helga was kind enough to pick her up at Frankfurt Airport and take care of her the rest of the way. Mutti liked to be waited on, she needed to be pampered. I trained myself to be the opposite, self-reliant and independent, more like my father.

December 1990 Mutti fell and was taken by ambulance to the hospital. I was called to come immediately and was told if she pulls thru she cannot live on her own any longer. She had become very forgetful and missed taking her medications frequently. Dementia! She had gone out for dinner every day and ate the same foods. She liked what she ate but it was a poor diet. What now? She told me several times she never wanted to live in America, she did not speak the language, or wanted to learn it, and she would not leave her sisters. Convincing Mutti to go to a rest-home, giving up her apartment, was not an easy task. The mental stress on me was horrendous, besides Christmas was only three weeks away.

She did get well enough to be moved to a semi-independent care facility. With the help of my good friend Klaus who had many business connections, I was able to locate a wonderful facility just down the street in Mutti's old neighborhood. The home had only 12 private rooms, all with private bath. It was managed and operated by catholic nuns.

There was a large garden, beautiful dining room and medication was distributed. Meals were served in your private room if necessary and doctors made private house calls. Luck was with me, as a room had just become available. No time to waste, I had to act. I signed the papers for the available room immediately. I knew she would receive excellent care and she was able to come and go as she pleases, sit in the gardens and go for walks. Her favorite restaurant the "Buerger Spital" was across the street and she was still able to spend time there with her sisters, eating dinner in or out and drinking her favorite glass of wine.

I cancelled the lease on her apartment and made arrangement to sell many of her worldly possessions. I had to sort thru all her personal items, her clothes etc. and select all her necessary items that would go to her new address. I also ordered a large shipping container to pack things up to ship to America. She wanted me to take everything, especially her most valuable items, including the oil paintings. I sold lots of household items, donated many things to charity and threw out a lot. Many items I put out on the curb for city pick up. I waited and waited, the stuff did not get picked up. After making several phone calls I learned that I needed to purchase special trash bags to get rid of things. It was costly for the city to dispose of items, so purchasing these special bags paid for the cost of taking refuge away. I re-packed the trash bags and did it their way.

Remember, I had only three weeks from the time I got to Germany till Christmas. I came down with a debilitating migraine headache. I did not know if I was coming or going. Stress was taking over and destroying me. I called my husband on the phone and broke down. I remember sitting on the floor and crying in the midst of people wanting to purchase furniture. Within two days, Doug arrived to give me mental support. It was not an easy task for him to get vacation time in December from the Post office.

I did it all, emptied and cleaned the apartment. It was shiny, spotless and in perfect condition, just the way my mother would have wanted it to be, to hand over the keys to a new owners. I sat on the floor on Oegg Strasse #1 and had another breakdown, after all I was leaving the home where I stayed in on all my visits. All was gone now. No more home in Germany. It was more emotional for me that time than when I had left the first time. I called the travel agent and asked her "just book a flight for my husband and I to fly back to the USA so we will be home in time for Christmas". I did not care what day we would travel. Mutti was settling in, not without disagreements but she could understand that this decision was the only solution. I don't think she understood that this was now her new permanent home. She thought she was going back to her apartment someday soon.

Being an only child puts all the decision making on me. I was prepared for that, but it was very stressful. I always had to make the decisions. I had to take charge again and it had to be done fast. It was so difficult. This is all I could do and I was beginning to lose it again. The migraine took over again and I was a mess.

We were booked on PAN AM flight 103 for Dec. 19, 1988. Finally on the plane. Calm down, that's what I told myself. The weather became very stormy across the English Channel, not uncommon for that time of year. The plane appeared to be very old and rattled continuously. Food and drink service was halted and delayed for a while. It came to mind that this plane was not going to withstand the storm. I occupied myself by reading the PAN AM "Clipper Magazine", always one of my favorites and I stashed it in my hand luggage for a keepsake. We did land in one piece and I was so glad we could get home to be with our boys for the holidays. The boys surprised us with a perfectly decorated Christmas tree, which unfortunately had tipped over by the time we had gotten home. Most of my new glass ornaments (which I just had purchased in 1990 at the closeout sale at Sibley's department store) were broken.

Oh well, it can always get worse – and it did.

In the morning of Dec. 21st, 1988 I tried to put my tree back together when my husband called from work and asked me to sit down. Honey, the PAN AM flight 103, the same plane we flew the other day, just crashed over Scotland. No survivors! Immediately I shouted out to him, "I told you so, the plane was not safe, it was too old and should not have been in service", the plane could not withstand another stormy flight.

PAN AM flew back to Frankfurt on the 20th and did the regular scheduled flight from Frankfurt to destination Detroit via London on the 21st. A bomb exploded killing all 243 passengers and the crew of 16. It became known as the Lockerbie bombing. I was speechless and shocked. How could this happen and how lucky are we that the agent booked us for the 19th. She had suggested the 21st but I insisted to get home as soon as possible.

Fate? Luck? Merry Christmas to us all! The whole country was in mourning.

My mother adapted to her new surroundings quite well until her death in February 1994. I visited her twice every year and took care of all her needs for six month in advance. She had a small wooden box with a key and I put enough cash in there to last her till my next visit. Every Sunday at 8 am I would ring her, her time being 1 pm in the afternoon. She always asked when I will come to see her, even when I just had left her two days before. Dementia!

Every Sunday we talked about the upcoming week and I told her how much spending money she needed to take from the box to put in her small wallet. She enjoyed drinking her Steh-coffee (stand-up coffee, very popular in Europa) and she indulged in a piece of Torte, a special treat. She also insisted on buying a daily newspaper. She read the same newspaper at least twice a day without needing reading glasses. By afternoon she had forgotten what she read in the morning, so it was always news to her. She also gave lots of coins to the homeless sitting on most every street corner in Wuerzburg. She made sure she always had enough coins for each beggar in her pocket. She enjoyed sharing and giving. "They need to eat too" was her answer.

Hair appointments, manicure and pedicures, I scheduled ahead for the next six month and paid for in advance. She could walk to all her appointments, nice to live in the city. Everybody in the neighborhood knew her and that was comforting to me. She had her routine.

She passed away having a brain aneurysm after spending four years in the assisted living home. I could not fly over in time to say good bye to her but was there to make arrangements for a proper funeral.

For the last time I packed things up including lots of memories. This was my final good bye, I knew it will never be the same again. I made one last stroll thru my City by myself, I said goodbye and made peace with myself. So beautifully re-built after the bombing, like nothing ever happened. In the years to come, I flew back to Germany every other year, visiting with my cousin Helga and her family.

Being homesick got better over the years living in America, the holidays will always be emotional. Life will never be perfect, I learned that early on. I either missed my parents in Germany, or I missed my own family in America. There was no perfect solution, there is always something missing. Your heart is always half here and half there.

"You make your bed – and you lay in it".

In 1992 Doug and I had taken a trip back to Germany for a very special re-union with members of the 10th Division Band. The City of Wuerzburg had invited all the band members for a special visit to thank the American Army band for establishing such a special relationship between the people of Wuerzburg and the American military. The Mayor of Wuerzburg wined and dined us at city hall and we got a special tour of the Rathaus with its beautiful meeting hall and tower, the city hall I was married in. We climbed up the many stairs to the very top of the tower, where replicas are displayed, one of the city of Wuerzburg before 1945 and one after 1945.

I looked at both replicas and all of a sudden I lost it. I started to cry, I was shaking and sobbing and Doug had to walk me out of this small tower room to sit on a bench. All the memories of the bombings came back, it hit me like a ton of bricks. I usually can hide my emotions but was not able to this time. I still have a difficult time thinking and writing about these memories.

That trip, for the first time in my life, I almost felt like a tourist. Being with the other band members was special. We took boat tours on the Rhein and Main, visited the famous wine towns along both rivers. Great time being a tourist.

After my parents passing I found my life in the US more acceptable and adaptable, it became easier. This a very strange thing to say. While my parents were alive, not ever did a Sunday go by when I did not call to Germany at 8 o'clock in the morning. We always kept up the communications, I miss that very much.

After 25 years of working at the Post Office, Doug was able to retire. He was 55 and looking forward to have some freedom in his life. He still played music but not as passionate as in the earlier days. Rock'n Roll was not his preferred choice of music, the demographics of music had changed. He always was and would be a "Jazz" musician.

He decided to buy himself a Liquor store (not the building) in the Hamlet of Cheshire to occupy himself a bit, or should I say a lot. It was different, but he enjoyed it. He could not draw his Military pension till age 60, so the Liquor store provided some income before he could collect his pension. After owning the store for five years the building was sold and we were out of business. Very unexpected, at a big loss financially.

Barbados

My Island In The Sun

For our 25th wedding anniversary, Doug and I afforded ourselves a trip to Barbados. We traveled with our good friends Art and Rita, a couple who emigrated from Germany in the late 1950's, approximately the same time I arrived in this country. We had become the best of friends over the years with similar backgrounds and lots in common. We also could speak and keep up the German language.

The flight from Rochester to Miami and onto the beautiful island of Barbados was uneventful. Arriving about 11 pm in the darkness, a taxi took us to our beachside hotel room. The clerk opened the door to our room, switched on the light and the first thing I saw was a two inch long cockroach on the wall. The critter seemed to be disturbed by our appearance and the sudden bright light. I freaked out and it was some time for my husband to convince me of their existence and better get used to it. Cockroaches call the islands their home, so it's their territory.

Next morning all was well when I awoke to a beautiful view of the white beach and the turquois sea. We swam in the warm water, laid on the beach, took tours of the island and did the touristy thing, all beautiful. We were asked to listen to a presentation for "Time share" opportunities and sales. All sounded well, we were exited and on the

3rd day we purchase a time share with "DIVI" Hotels. This allowed us an annual two week vacation on the beautiful island of Barbados. As a bonus the Management offered us two extra weeks per year which meant we could spend a total of four weeks per year in heaven. Our friends agreed to do the same thing, only to withdraw from this adventures opportunity several weeks later. Doug and I decided to keep the deal, it would force us to take a restful and lengthy vacation every year for the next 25 years. We are going to get our monies worth.

Within the first years of our trip to Barbados we became close friends with two couples, one from Scotland, Angus and Christine and the other couple, Ken and Iris, they called the UK their home. When we arrived on the island in "South Winds" lobby, we were greeted by the hotel management with rum punch and hors-d'oeuvres and of course our friends, the welcoming committee always ready and happy to see us. The six of us started to spend days and evenings together, enjoyed great meals in fabulous restaurant with steel bands playing Reggae music. We visited local entertaining shows and danced the evenings away. The Europeans are used to a much more formal evening routine, it was dress up time. No shorts on our dinner table. Dinner began with a "Starter" and the meals lasted several hours. I fell right into it, my European background was not lost. There are no late nights on the island, the evening routine starts about 6 pm, by 11 o'clock most everybody was in bed sound asleep.

The average temperature in Barbados is a very comfortable 82 degrees, that is pretty much year around and it does not cool down much at night. The little rain they get is mostly during the night.

I like to start my morning routine about 6 AM with a long walk on the beach or through the neighborhoods followed by a long swim in the Olympic sized pool. This was my alone time, a time to think, my happy time. Breakfast we enjoyed in our suite or on the balcony. The routine continued with sun bathing or swimming, sun tanning and/ or burning. In the early years I went to a tourist orientation seminar. The locals told us the "sun bites" between the hours from 11 o'clock in the morning till two in the afternoon. Good time to have lunch followed by a nap in the shade.

The six of us booked tours together, flew to other islands and had a marvelous time. I had some trouble understanding the English accent but found it even more difficult understanding the Scottish brogue. When Christine and Angus talked to each other, I needed a translator. They were heavy smokers as most Europeans are, so was my husband Doug. At least most of the smoking was done outdoors and I could tolerate it.

Several times our adult sons joined us for vacation and we were proud to show off our island in the sun. We had fun on the Jolly Rogers, where we jumped from the high rope into the sea, enjoyed ourselves doing the Congo line, singing "feeling hot, hot, hot, or "No woman, no cry". We hung out at Crane Beach, voted to be one of the best 10 beaches in the world. The rugged east coast is beautiful and there are many small fishing villages on the island.

The catamarans where always a favorite and so was the local transportation, shabby and very old small VW buses with reggae music blaring. Everybody had to sway in the same direction whether sitting or standing in the bus, otherwise we would not fit. The transportation, whatever it might be that day, was always filled to capacity. Shopping in Bridgetown, having lunch and visiting the "Colombian Emeralds" store were all my favorites. It was so much fun.

We have been doing these wonderful vacations for approximately ten years, never had much interest in trading and/or exchanging our location, visiting any place else. We loved Barbados and called it our second home.

At one of our evening dinners my husband started choking on his perfectly prepared steak dinner. This was the first time of such an incident, we promised our friends to get this checked out when we are back at home. That was 1993.

We made an appointment with our doctor shortly after we arrived back in Canandaigua. Our family doctor send us to a specialist in Geneva. After several visits with various doctors, the gruesome diagnose was esophageal cancer. He needed surgery as soon as possible. We cried together, we had no idea what we were in for. Eleven hours in surgery at FF Thompson hospital in Canandaigua with a one month hospital stay, then two more months at Strong Memorial with several more surgeries.

Our lives never were the same.

The next three years were a learning and life changing experience for both of us. Several more surgeries with lengthy hospital stays followed. 1995, almost two years into the disease, Doug decided he wanted one more visit to Barbados. I took lots of specialty foods along for him and we spent most of our time in our suite and on the balcony. Our friends helped out as much as they could. We only stayed two weeks, we knew it was his last time.

April 1996, Christine rang me from Barbados and gave me shocking news. Angus was sitting on a chair waiting for Christine getting ready for a dinner party. She heard a loud noise, Angus felt off the chair and was dead. The coroner was called and he was hauled off to the local morgue in Bridgetown. Massive heart attack was the verdict. Christine had to go to the morgue to identify her husband's body. She told me she did not have any trouble doing that, he was the only white body there. We laughed over this statement. The hotel staff and guests all were in shock.

May 24th 1996, Doug and I were blessed with new life, our first granddaughter was born. Doug got to hold and enjoy her for two months. He always wanted a girl. We celebrated Sydney's Christening July 21 with a big party at our house. We invited all of our friends. It was wonderful to enjoy the Christening and it was the perfect time for Doug's friends to enjoy a last visit with him and say good-bye.

July 30th 1996 my husband of 37 years passed away at age 62. I was prepared and ready to let him go. How long should anybody have to suffer? Condolences poured in from family and friends including from Ken and Iris from England and Christine from Scotland.

It was about October the same year, the phone rang from the UK. Iris gave me the terrible news that her husband of 30 years past away from a massive heart attack. All three husbands passed the same year. What the hell happened here? I cannot describe the feeling.

Each year thruout our long friendship I had remembered our friends Iris and Christine with Christmas. No return card from Christine. After several months I received an answer to my Christmas card from one of Christine's distant relatives (she had no children) informing me Christine had passed away from cancer in December 1996.

Oh what a year it was. Schicksal? Fate? I am in shock!

And the music stopped! It was a good time knowing you all.

Life tells me to move on.

The following spring Stuart, Seana and I traveled to Barbados. We carried a small box with half of Doug's ashes with us. For the last day of our vacation I made arrangements with a catamaran owner to meet us at the beach in the early morning. Unexpected, it was pouring rain, windy and blowing. The guy was a no-show. Desperately I walked the beach looking for a replacement to take us out to sea to do the heart breaking job to bury my husband at sea. My determination put all of us in a dangerous situation, but I needed to get this job done. We are here and it has to be done now and we went sailing. Stuart and Seana pushed the boat out into the open waters and the captain had a difficult time controlling the raft. I hung on for dear life, feeling the heavy rain drops on my bare skin, my blond hair flying in the strong winds. Stuart had a difficult time opening the zipper to the bag to open it to empty the ashes in the breeze. For a moment I was afraid he would go overboard. The ashes blew all over and ended up in the sea somewhere. Looking from the sea back to shore I recognized Christ Church, said a prayer and mumbled "rest in peace". I had an approximate location to focus on of his final resting place, "Christ Church in Barbados", the place he loved so much, his "happy place".

Barbados continued to be my happy place for many more years to come, till our "Time Share" expired.

It was the best thing while it lasted.

Barbados

Stuart and Seana

And Than The Music Stopped

My husband passed away at age 62 after a three year battle with cancer and being married to each other for 37 years. By the age of 57 I was widowed.

My sons were busy with their own lives. I started to switch to survival mode again. I have to be strong, I have to make a life for myself and guide my sons along during this life altering period. I did most of my grieving during the three years of Doug's illness. Derek, Stuart and Seana coming for dinner almost every Sunday, to visit with their father. Doug Jr. was living in Park City, Utah at the time but communicated with his father every week.

Doug and Renata

Renata and her Sons

I had taken charge of all doctor's appointments, I sat in the waiting rooms and hospital rooms for hours. The care, the worries. I was told he could live from three days to three years. Three surgeries, three hospital stays, the longest almost four months at Strong Memorial in Rochester. It was almost three years to the day when he passed. Most every morning on my early walk I cried my eyes out, nobody ever saw me do that. To all my friends I appeared "strong" It was my way of dealing with his illness and preparing myself for a future without him. I considered it a blessing being able to take care of him for three years.

He never wanted to talk about death or dying but one evening I was brave enough to ask.

"What gives you the will and strength to live"?

"Oh, you do, you take such good care of me", was his answer.

"What do you want me to do after you're gone?" His simple answer:

"You'll figure it out".

As far as he was concerned I can handle it all and deal with it. I prepared myself to let him go, three years is a long time to see your loved one suffer.

It was a dreadful summer. I did not know if I was coming or going.

The only wonderful thing for Doug and I was having our first grandchild arrive in May, what a joy. Doug was able to celebrate her birth and even made a trip on his own to the hospital to welcome Sydney. He was thrilled to have her for a short time.

Sydney's christening party on July 21, 1996 was a big celebration. It was a combination of celebrating our new granddaughter into the world and celebrating Doug's life. A perfect summer day, guests enjoyed meeting our beautiful grandchild and saying goodbye to Doug. He passed nine days later.

A hospice nurse helped us out during the last few weeks of his life. She recommended I keep doing my early morning walks and keep up with my Real Estate business, the best I can. The aide was a big fan of stock-car racing and so was Doug. The two had something in common and had fun conversations. It made me feel good that they bonded. The day we agreed to put a hospital bed into our bedroom, (the boys put it all together), Doug gave up. He made sure he talked with each of his sons that very same day. Our son Doug was living in Park City, they had their last conversation. Derek, Stuart and Seana dismantled the hospital bed that very same night and put it in the garage to return it the next day to the rental store.

Back to work as soon as possible, that's what I did. I did most anything to distract myself. Keep busy.

My Second Chance At Love And Life

I worked in my Real Estate office mostly with the door closed to catch up with my work. It was September now and a very busy time for me. A new Real Estate Broker had joined our office during the summer months, having moved from North Carolina to Canandaigua. I met him briefly walking into the office but did not have time to welcome him. After several weeks of friendly "Hello's and "Good Byes" he - very delicately – asked if I would consider joining him for lunch. I accepted without hesitation. After all, a girl has to eat.

I was at a most vulnerable state and so was he, being newly divorced.

Well, it was lunch only.

Richard was a cheerful, nice looking gentleman, pleasant to be with. He kept pursuing me and within a few months we established a comfortable relationship. I was not looking for a male companion ship, he just happened to find me. My original plan for the future was taking some time for myself, not having to care and deal with anybody. I wanted to figure things out on my own, learn how to operate the TV control and run my life. I was going to watch my choice of TV programs, (not sports). So very selfish of me.

Why did the good Lord send him my way? I talked with my sons about it, their answer was, "it's too early Mom, but you know best!"

I did not know anything about Richard, he was new in town, just moved back from another State. Was he for real or a criminal preying on a new lonely widow, was he as good as he appeared to be?

I agree I had my doubts and questioned myself continuously. What am I doing? After all it has only been a few months since my husband passed away but I also recognized I have been grieving for the last three years while Doug was seriously ill. I was ready to move on and Richard picked me up in my darkest days and hours.

I must admit he did not come without a past. He had three marriages behind him; that made me stop and think. He had four adult children. I decided from the start I was not going to be wife number four, being independent was my goal. It took some adjusting getting used to a new man but he turned out to be the most caring and unselfish person I have ever known. He is kind, loving and generous and totally committed to our relationship. Together we moved from respect to adoration and love. We fell in love and we are deeply committed to each other.

Life is never perfect, but it can come close. We are two totally different personalities with different backgrounds. It is very different when two young people fall in love and build a life and future side by side and grow together. In our more mature years we are set in our ways, people are molded and established, we know what we want and our past is very much entwined in our future.

We have been together for more than 26 years now, mostly very good and wonderful times. It has been a very interesting journey and a very serious and solid relationship. We never married. We always retained our own homes, which was and still is very important to me. I have grown into a very independent person. I learned to take care of myself, however it is wonderful to have the right person beside you to share life with. To share the good and the not so good, the fun times and to bounce off each other the small and the big problems.

I feel very much appreciated. He loves to spoil me. He has never forgotten to acknowledge an occasion. My family loves him and the grand kids consider him the Grandpa they did not have. I remained the feisty one, the survivor. He loves doing for people, trying to make everybody happy. Richard definitely turned out to be a keeper. We are happy together.

Richard has a good since of humor, always a twinkle in his eye. We laugh a lot and he loves surprises. He is a genius with numbers and loves negotiations. He also can sell a refrigerator to an Eskimo. I have a little more common sense and I am more skeptical. I feel I got the edge on him being the practical one. I am not a dreamer. We worked in the same agency side by side till Richard decided to purchase the business. It became "Bristol Hills Realty" and we kept working together for about nine years.

We thought of marriage several times, it would not have lasted. I did not feel like being number four. I am glad I recognized that early on. We both are enjoying our independence - together.

I had never lived on my own before, so I wanted to experience that. Being in a comfortable financial situation helped a lot. I also enjoyed my job very much. We called ourselves "domestic partners". Over the years, we shared so much fun, love and comfort. We are sharing our lives together, every trip, vacations, all the celebrations and graduations, and we are still enjoying it all – in sickness and in health.

We made many beautiful trips to Barbados, different islands in the Caribbean. We travelled to Mexico, Alaska and California. Many trips we made to Germany to visit relatives with side tours to Osterreich (Austia) and Prag. We visited Budapest, Wien and other beautiful cities on a Viking River tour. Went out west to see Vancouver in Canada, Butchart Gardens in British Columbia. Each trip was more fun than the other. We wintered for many years in Florida, calling "The Villages" our winter home.

I continued living on West Lake Road along with "My Piano". It was my secure home with all the comforts I could afford including a park-like back yard and a kidney shaped swimming pool. We had picnics there, my three grandchildren enjoyed the wild life including lots of deer, who hung out in the backyard. They peeked in the window, roamed in the spacious yard and ate from the apple trees.

Over the years I got to know Richard's family and we have shared and enjoyed many visits and vacations together. Richard has six beautiful grandchildren.

Stuart and Seana blessed me with two more grandchildren, besides Sydney, I have Henry who was born in 1999 and Reilly in 2002. Beautiful children, little Henry and a sweet girl named Reilly. I enjoy them so much and I am so proud to be their "Oma".

Christmas always was a special time, my home was the place to gather and celebrate all the holidays. Cooking and entertaining was fun, it made me happy. Getting the family together was our enjoyment. The big house and yard with pool was a lot of work and in the later years most of the labor was hired out. I continued to work as a Real Estate Broker, I was able to pick my own working hours and it suited me well. I specialized marketing Bed &Breakfast in Up State NY besides marketing residential properties in our area.

My 70th birthday – 70 years old. Quite an accomplishment I thought.

I am still living on West Lake Road.

It is a beautiful day, warming up already at 6 am. I am taking an early walk. This is my daily routine and I love it. It is very special to me so, I meditate, get my thoughts together and thank the Lord for a very good life. I think about Doug who made it only to age 62 years of age. That puts a damper on things. Once at home, I mulch the flower beds. The pool will be opened today, always lots of work. The Happy Birthday wishes are starting to arrive, many phone calls including calls from Germany.

Go to work, first appointment cancelled. A beautiful bouquet from Rich (Richard's son) and his wife Roxanne arrives. I have lunch with my longtime friend Ursel at "Inn on the Lake". We are enjoying the wonderful sunshine on the deck, a glass of wine. Looks like a perfect day for a birthday celebration. Back to work, pick up Reilly from school, I take her to ballet lessons. She has problems getting her hair into a bun, she does not talk to me, Reilly is miffed. Not my fault. Richard comes to pick me up, he had made dinner reservations with our friends Don and Lois at "Richardson's Canal House" Pittsford/ Bushnell's Basin to celebrate my big birthday. I order duck for dinner, delicious.

My wonderful Richard explains to me that my birthday present did not fit in the car, so he got me a miniature sized present. A travel book for a River Cruise on the Donau, (Danube) to Budapest, cruising back to Nuernberg, Wuerzburg and flying back home from Amsterdam. How lovely, a huge surprise. I am so thrilled and exited, thank you my Love!

The following Saturday, we made plans to go out for dinner to celebrate my birthday with my family. I am only told to dress up. I am watching the Kentucky Derby on the TV, they are just about ready to start the race when the doorbell rings. "Your chariot is here, Madam". A white stretch limo with the license plate 1939 is in my "what appeared to be a very small", driveway. "I cannot go now, I have to watch the end of the Derby", I said. All my family was waiting for me in the limo to take me to the "Woodcliff" for special celebration. My very first Limo ride at age 70! A wonderful, very special surprise. Everybody in a terrific, joyful mood. The grandkids adorable, my pride and joy. I ordered lamb, we drink" Opus One" wine, we dance twice, the band played "Happy Birthday" for me. Colorful spring flowers on the table, many great presents. A birthday cake with seven candles. My family pulled it off! I am so lucky!

The summer of 2009 is moving along. Richard is moving in with me for the interim, since he sold his house at Bristol Harbor rather quickly. He is a pack-rat and needs to get rid of a lot of stuff. He is building a new house in the "Villas" in Canandaigua, just around the corner where I eventually will move to.

And another big birthday this year. Richard is turning 75. I am planning a surprise birthday party for him at the Community Center at Bristol Harbor. Pork Bar BQ is on the menu, about 55 people, Scott K. is playing the piano and Vicky B. (Richard's niece) is singing for him. So much fun, a huge success.

The following month we spent a week on Bald Head Island, NC with all of Richard's family. A ferry took us from the main land to the small island. A beautiful vacation house on the beach accommodated the extended large B. family. We had the opportunity to watch Loggerhead turtles hatch around midnight. Very interesting for young and old. A big crowd gathered around midnight seeing the hatchlings on their first walk to the sea.

October 7th 2009, European vacation with River cruise on the Donau, (Danube)

For three days we enjoyed Budapest. We had reservations staying at the Kaminski Hotel for three nights, quite an experience by itself. The hotel is old but very luxurious. The shower room was as large as my bedroom at home with large ceramic tiles, even on the ceiling..

Budapest is such a beautiful city with so much to see, all beyond my expectations. We listened to Gypsy music, ate Goulash and did the touristy thing, including going to the Roman baths. We walked and walked and walked. Wish I could do that now.

The River Cruise was a great experience, every day a fantastic memory. We did all the excursions that were offered, especially enjoyed Wien. Toured Schloss Schoenbrunn and also got to see the Lippensteiner Horses. We left the tour boat in Nuernberg.

My cousin Gerd and wife Else met us in Nuernberg. They came to the river boat with a large bouquet of flowers to welcome us. Germans are so hospitable to their guests and it was a joy to stay with them. We had the use of their beautiful guest suite for our stay of four days.

We toured Nuernberg with them, Richard had never seen the city before. Of course we ate local cuisine, mostly "Nuernberger Bratwuerstle", (a specialty) in the well known and popular restaurants, we toured the "Burg", the world famous Nuernburger fortress located in the center of the city. It was an experience, even for me. I had seen the city many times before, however, seeing Nuernberg as a tourist was different.

Later on that week Gerd and Else drove us to Wuerzburg and we spent 10 days in my home town. We stayed with Helga and Helmut in their lovely villa, visited with Aunts and Uncles. Not too many left but I made it a point to visit every one of my relatives still alive. I arranged to meet with a few old school chums in a restaurant. Great time reminiscing and sharing good and bad memories. There are still a few school chums around, very old friends.

Our next stop was Amsterdam. We took the train from Wuerzburg, had a very luxurious train ride in 1st class to Amsterdam. Huge train station. Richard always books a hotel room in the center of the city, so we asked the taxi driver to take us to our hotel called "Golden Tulip".

We were told there are about 29 "Golden Tulips" in Amsterdam and our reservation happened to be the "The Golden Tulip" hotel on the outskirts of the city. What a bummer! Several miles from City Center. We took the trolley every day to see the museums, the canals and waterways and especially enjoyed watching the local folks riding and maneuvering their bicycles everywhere. We took a bus tour to Dan Haag, saw the Delph factory make porcelain and watched Hollanders make cheese somewhere. . We viewed the night life in the daytime including the "Red Light District" and absolutely enjoyed our last days in Europe.

Time to go home, we've been gone for a month and bringing back memories of a lifetime.

Richard

A Trip With Reilly

July 2014

This will be my last trip to Germany.

We are taking my youngest granddaughter Reilly with us. I am 75 and generally in good health. Richard will celebrate his 80 birthday in August. We are scheduled to leave for Germany on July 30th. Reilly will celebrate her 12th birthday on the trip. She is very bright and hopefully will have good memories with her Oma. I had invited Sydney and Henry also, they declined. Sydney being too busy with College preparations for St. John Fisher College and Henry, 15 years old, going thru puberty and is not comfortable in his own skin. He is doing sports this summer, keeping busy with ball games but really nothing very constructive.

This time we are staying with Cousin Helga's daughter Uschi. She also lives in Gerbrunn like her parents. She owns a beautiful three story home. Helga and Helmut are getting on in age and three people for company is a bit much for them. They did come to spend every day with us and visited, they live within walking distance. Helmut showed Reilly all the "Sehenswuerdigkeiten" - points of interest - in and around Wuerzburg. Again we walked, walked and walked and talked.

Helga and I did a lot of reminiscing and all the old stories come back to life. We talk about our families, specially our parents and of course the war. How different life has turned out for each of us. She has a great marriage to Helmut and they have two daughters. They built their own home and both daughters have two children. I am happy to say, everything turned out well for them. Helmut started his career at age 14, delivering mail on his bicycle and worked his way up to Postmaster managing the largest Post office in Wuerzburg. He did very well for himself, is extremely bright and should have been an engineer. Unfortunately, the opportunity after the war was not available.

I pulled off a very small family reunion. Cousin Erwin surprised us with a visit with his lovely wife Hannelore. He had immigrated to Switzerland shortly after the war. So sorry I never got to visit him there, we had drifted apart. I had lost contact with Erwin for 65 years. I so very much regret that we never got together in our earlier years when we were more mobile. It was super exiting exchanging our life stories with each other.

Reilly was a big help on the trip and in the airports, she could read the directional signs much faster than us old folks. She also was able to lift some heavy suitcases which we could not do. At first she was not excited about German food but many times she commented "this is the best steak I ever tasted, or this is the best of this and that". She did have a good time meeting her cousins, it was a whole new experience for her. We flew first class and introduced her to a more comfortable way of travel, she was very excited and enjoyed the flight in comfort and luxury. On the plane we each had our own cabin with pull-out beds, she probably watched four movies and communicated on her iPad with all her girlfriends. We flew back on her actual birthday and the pilot invited her into the cock-pit. She was even more excited about that.

I cherished this last visit and I decided it was my last trip to Germany.

I simply cannot say "Good Bye" again and again. It is so hard when you know it might be the last time that you see your relatives and your home country. All good things come to an end.

When I watched the train rolling into the train station in Wuerzburg, the tears started to flow. Powerful emotions, I experienced too many times.

A Trip with Reilly arriving Wuerzburg

At the Train station in Wuerzburg

We had a wonderful trip, visiting with the few remaining relatives. My emotions just run too high and as my mother said, at the very beginning of my journey, "you make your bed and you lay in it". Time to move on.

In 2016 I sold the house on West Lake Road and build a new residence in a retirement community called "The Villas of Canandaigua" only one mile away from my old home and best of all, only a few houses away from Richard's home. Lovely neighborhood, heated community swimming pool, close to hospital and all medical facilities and only two miles from Wegmans, our very popular grocery store. Perfect.

Do I have room for the piano? Do I need to build a home large enough to accommodate the piano? I quickly remembered that the purpose to move is get a smaller home and cut down on maintenance.

Sydney decided she wants her piano. Fine with me, but where will it go. Stuart and Seana agreed to take the piano and park it in their living room for the interim time, till Sydney has a home of her own. Stuart and Seana's living room is rectangular in shape and the piano will fit between two build-in book cases. It fits fine and enhances to room.

When the children were little, Seana had purchased an old upright piano for the kids to play on, none of them ever learned how to play an instrument. That old upright is still taking up space, nobody plays. The only house with two pianos in the same room, both silent.

Sydney hopes, some day in the future she will have children and they will learn how to play the old piano. I hope so too!!!

Some day she will claim the piano and her grandfather will be delighted.

Our Golden Years

2018

This is the fourth year we are spending the winter in Florida in a retirement community called "The Villages". Richard rented a beautiful house.

Just before we left NY I was diagnosed with Tennis – elbow. This turned into a very painful and complicated problem. Could not use my right arm for almost eight months, not able to drive the car, do my hair and. Just try to put on a swimsuit with one hand. Doing everything with the left hand is complicated when you're right handed. Therapy twice a week and with no improvements. To top off our dilemma, the first night at our vacation home, Richard fell out of bed. I heard a loud noise, looked over and Richard had disappeared. He rolled himself right out of bed. The X-rays showed some cracked ribs. We are a good pair, both injured on our vacation. Everything was a struggle, but we managed. We drove the golf cart to the pool and enjoyed ourselves the best we could.

We had lots of company visiting us, my two granddaughters Sydney and Reilly, Richard's granddaughter Maddie, Richard's son and his family, my son Doug and his new found love Karen. Our friends Cor and Diane and Richard's brother Doug and Brenda also stayed with us for several days. Of course they did not come at the same time and everybody was helpful. We were happy to see them and had a good time going to the square watching other people dance. They all pitched in to help.

Our stay in Florida was not the best with all our health issues. I decided, driving the car home was not an option for me. March 30th I flew home, Richard's brother Doug offered to drive the car and Richard back home to NY. I was looking forward to getting back to NY, seeing my family and sleeping in my own bed. All of a sudden I am feeling my age and I need a vacation from my vacation. This is probably my last Florida stay.

It's always been fun spending winters in Florida and leaving the snow behind in Upstate New York. I enjoyed the warmth and the sun, I experienced life in the "The Villages", with its many golf courses and upscale life style. I think pickle ball is the main sport there. You should never get bored in "The Villages" and you can be as secluded as you like, or busy, if you prefer. An abundance of great restaurants, two beautiful pools to every neighborhood; (and there are many) life entertainment is provided every evenings in each "Square" and the shopping is most enjoyable with lots of smaller boutiques. We are spending lots of time with our friends Jim and Karol, who originally introduced us to "The Villages" and showed us around. Our very special friends Cor and Diane always came to visit from Sun City, Florida and stayed for several days. We also got to see Richard's brother Doug and wife Brenda and we visited them several times at their home in Sun City Center.

Sydney graduated from St. John Fisher college school of nursing. She is now an RN and started her first job at RGH in Rochester. There also is a "steady" boyfriend in her life and she lives in the city. So proud of her. She has a plan, she has her life mapped out. So far, so good. She turned into a beautiful young woman and her life is on track and beginning to take shape. Love you so much, Sydney!

Henry decided to enter SUNY Potsdam in 2019. He is playing Lacrosse and is enjoying sports more than his studies. He is a very good looking young man, tall and muscular and I hope and pray he will find his way. Love you so much, Henry!

Summer is over. My right arm is in much better condition since Dr. M. injected Cortisone in early August. It helped a lot. I am typing again but don't want to overdue. Enjoyed the swimming exercise all summer. The pool was wonderful, an activity I really enjoy. I look forward to swimming, unfortunately cannot keep my commitment every day. Nice friendly ladies too, that makes it fun and entertaining. Lots of laughs, everybody has a story to tell. Since we are all newcomers to "The Villas in Canandaigua" we are still getting acquainted.

We did not do much this summer, mostly doctor's visits with Richard. My tooth is still bothering me, really would like to get it pulled.

I decided on my 2nd hip replacement and chose a surgeon located in Rochester. The waiting list is four months for an appointment and another several more months before scheduling surgery.

Finally, I took time to take pictures of my oil paintings and sent them off to Switzerland. Cousin Erwin said he would try to get an estimate from an art dealer in Bern. Let's wait and see!

Derek had promised Sydney a trip to Paris after she graduates from College. Well, this week they left for Paris. Wonderful. I am very excited for them. Derek has not had a vacation in more than 10 years and Syd is ready to start exploring the world. They sent beautiful pictures on Facebook every day. Looks like they are having a marvelous time. Somehow I see myself in Sydney, young, of course more beautiful than I ever was, the fire burning inside. She is ambitious, interested and ready to embrace the world.

This is the year I decided to retire, 2018. The pressure is off. The Rochester Real Estate Board rewarded me with a nice plaque "REALTOR EMERITUS" forty cumulative years of membership in the National Association for Realtors. Something to be proud of. No gold watch!

Funny, I thought I would miss the Real Estate Business. It turned out better than that, I never looked back. I will miss the very few agents I worked with, however no deep relationships were ever formed and I don't have many friends. My family always took priority and always will be my main focus. And I have Richard. Thank God for him!

My hip is really starting to give me trouble and I have to quit all pleasure walking. Not good, since walking around the block is one of my enjoyments. I am going full force with preparations for hip replacement surgery in February. Richard still would like to go south sometime this winter, I don't think it will happen.

Looks like Doug and Karen are in a relationship and I am happy he found an amazing woman and new love. They adore each other. They came to visit from Florida this fall. It was good to see them together. She is a very bubbly, talk- a- mile a minute and there is never a dull moment with her, lots of fun.

Doug inherited the musical talent from his father. Lots of compassion and feelings, he also has perfect pitch. All through his school years he played the Violin, later graduated to String Bass and guitar. He went to "All State" competition in High School and played bass in musical events with his Dad. I always hoped he would choose a career in music but he did not.

2018 is winding down. I feel old, waited too long for this hip replacement. Procrastination! I am limping and I tire easily. Richard also is in a lot of pain, his body is giving out. His hearing is bad, he is checking out hearing aids. After he got them, he won't wear them. I take him to Doctors, blood tests, massage and acupuncture. Nothing seems to work or help. Visited with Fr. David at St. John's Episcopalian church to make his final arrangements and set appointment to see Funeral director Jim Johnson. He thought it would make him feel better putting his final arrangements and business in order. I am very upset about this but try to keep my humor. We laugh about it together. It is all part of life. I agree that I need to do the same, but honestly, don't have the energy at this point.

What will I do without him, I ask this question often. We love each other so much and he supports me in every way. He does not deserve all this pain. Such a good compassionate person, a big part of my life. Actually, he is my life. It feels like the beginning of the end.

2019

Looks like a rough year ahead. Found a new dentist. Replaced crown that was put on by Dr. C. with new crown. Dr. J. my new dentist, called it a very ill-fitting crown. I was referred to the next Dentist, a young attractive lady from Nicaragua, she sent me to another dentist to have a tooth extracted. Last week I felt a painful sensation on my left site upper tooth. The new specialist, Dr. J. makes an apt. for me with Dr. D. Two days later I have Endodontic Surgery. Not a pleasant experience, in the chair for one hour and 15 min. Stiches in the gums and soft diet for a week. Tomorrow the stiches will be removed. I don't know how much money I spent on this tooth, plus the pain, the time and I end up having it pulled. Are you confused? I am. Seems like I have a new specialist for every tooth.

All this dental work had to be done before February 6th, when my hip replacement was scheduled at hospital in Rochester. I choose Dr. D. over Dr. M. he does a different procedure called the "Arteria Approach". Recovery supposedly is faster and easier.

The plan is to go to Clark Meadow for re-habilitation after my hospital stay. It is a re-habilitation facility, connected to and part of Ferris-Hill. They offer 24 hour care plus three tasty meals a day. Richard will be able to join me for the evening meal, so all was well.

Stuck in the house because of the snow storm, I am cooking and preparing meals ahead, sorting my things to take to take with me to the hospital and basically preparing myself mentally for the upcoming surgery.

The day finally arrived, February 6, 2019 - have to be at the hospital in Rochester at 5:30 am. Stuart is driving me. I told Alexa to wake me at 4:00 a.m. also Siri and Richard did call at 4 am.

After I showered, I load my car with my small case and the aluminum walker and drive to pick up Stuart. He will be driving my car while I am laid up. We decided Richard will drive to the hospital mid-morning, the approximate time when my surgery is completed. The day would have been way too long for him and the weather was not good either.

The wait in the overfull pre-surgery room was not long, anxious folks awaiting their turn. They swabbed my nose, I was told I am the only one in OR with germs. But, I am the important one. A spinal injection and anesthetic put me in La La land.

Wake up in recovery room, no recollection of anything. Nurses transport me upstairs to a private room which is very small. Large enough to move the bed and add some more equipment. Lots of things are being moved around. Lots of meds but very little narcotics. Extra strength Tylenol seems to be their choice of pain medication. I remember from my first hip replacement a morphine pump was given for self-administration. It was removed after a few days and I was more comfortable with that kind of pain control.

Lots of pain, I need lots of help getting in and out of bed. Nurses o.k. not too compassionate, food o.k. I did not have the strength to open all these plastic containers and be self-sufficient. Not much help or assistance from the nurses or technicians, so most of the time I did not eat. Should have hired a private nurse or someone to advocate for me. I should have thought of that earlier.

First time I stepped out of bed I was immediately aware that my right leg is longer than the left. Just reversed from the last hip replacement. Dr. D. had promised to correct the length of my leg, so he over corrected it. So terribly disappointed in this outcome, now with all the pain I have, I am totally confused and already disappointed with the outcome of this surgery.

The second day at the Hospital I developed a bad pain in the lower part of my esophagus/ stomach area. Finally at 4:00 p.m. they take me to X-rays. The Tylenol pills I was given by the nurse were quite large (I have a narrow esophagus) and got dislodged in my esophagus causing the pain. The pills just sat there till dissolved, not a pleasant experience. I am not a pill taker, prefer pain meds in liquid form. Dr. D. kept me for an extra day and discharged me on Saturday.

Seana and Reilly picked me up the next morning and drove me to "Clark Meadow" where I am to rest up for a week before released on my own. Everybody was extremely helpful, I sat in back seat of the car with my leg up.

The room at "Clark Meadow" is very nice and with good furniture. The bathroom is large with a shower stall and a chair to sit in the shower. A very comfortable recliner for me to rest in and several chairs for my guests comfort are placed in the room. The staff was extra nice and I managed to walk with a walker to the dining room for three wonderful meals each day.

Richard had left for Virginia on Saturday for three days, it was good for him to get away and I could concentrate on my rehabilitation and not worry about him. He was not in best of shape and is worrying me greatly.

Not enough good can I say about "Clark Meadow". When first walking to dining room I saw familiar faces, I saw people I have seen before in my community, some distant acquaintances which became friendly immediately. People came to welcome me and were hoping I made this my new home, a permanent move. Not so fast here.

Lucky me, I got to leave and go home at the end of the week. When Richard came back from VA he joined me every evening for supper and enjoyed getting familiar with the compound. We loved the meals which we selected off the menu, small portions, well prepared and just the way we enjoy it. All was good, thank you Richard. I did experience being old, living in "Assisted Living" quarters. This is what the future looks like? Realization is setting in. In two months I will turn 80. Yes, I have to admit, this is old age and I need to accept something most of us don't want to deal with. The clock is ticking and NOT turning back. I am joining a different group of people.

There is a good side to this, younger folks open the door for me and are more courteous. So, there are advantages in getting older, I am trying to look at the bright side. These are the bonus years I am telling myself.

Once at home I had a visiting nurse and physical therapist, they kept me moving in the right direction.

Had my six week check up with a Nurse-Practitioner at the hospital yesterday. All is well except for right leg being longer than the left. Not much I can do about it, I have to accept it. I guess I could sue the Doctor/hospital. I don't have the strength for that and by the time it would be over, I would be dead anyway. How could this happen? The 2nd time? Only this time the left leg is shorter. I just cannot win.

I am done with Re-hab.

It is the end of April and still snowing. April came in like a lamb and is going out like a lion. My 80th birthday is just around the corner and I am getting nervous. My six months check-up was yesterday with my primary physician. I decided there are too many things wrong with me to even mention. He only has 10 minutes to spend with me. I believe the time management might be dictated by the insurance company. Hardly enough time to say hello and good bye. He doesn't seem to be too concerned. Just take another pill or take only one where you been taking two, does not seem to help. Also added a Cardiologist to my medical team, nice young lady. I was diagnosed with too many PVC's (heart beats) I figured better too many than not enough. But it wears out your heart, even so I feel pretty good. Oh well! I have to die of something.

Richard and Renata

My Bonus Years

I always said, any year over 80 is a bonus year. Well, I am at that point. My birthday worried me a bit, nobody mentions anything. I am sure the boys are planning something. Perhaps a surprise. I don't like surprises. Always like to be prepared and in control of a situation. It feels odd. Nobody is saying a word. Maybe I should just go away and surprise them with my absence. I think Doug and Karen are coming. It feels almost like they are avoiding me. I said to Richard, maybe we should just ask a few friends over for Monday, the 13th, after all I will turn 80 only once. I like to be somewhat in control and don't like to act surprised and be thankful for something I might not like. Oh well, we shall see. I should not worry about anything, my kids will do the right thing.

My 80's BIRTHDAY

Doug and Karen arrived on a Thursday. My sons and Richard surprised me with the most elaborate birthday celebration any one can imagine. By 4:00 o'clock on Sunday I still did not know what to wear, since I don't know where I am going. My ride arrives and I think we will drive to Geneva, "Belhurst" was my expectation. Many cars are parked at our Activity Center here at the "Villas" but I still don't get it. Well, we pull in the Activity Center and people yell "Happy Birthday, Happy Birthday" Mom. We are here. There must be 80 people inside the Center, (some I did not really know), live music is playing. Richard shows me this beautiful and very unusual birthday cake, a design copied from a McKenzie Childs design, called Courtly Check. It was gorgeous and of course it was Richard's idea. It was the best surprise party ever, perfectly orchestrated, all for me and in my honor. Hard to believe and I am stunned. Catered dinner by Eric's office. Champagne with personalized champagne glasses with my name and birth day engraved. It was a fabulous surprise and wonderful party. Derek, Doug, Stuart and Richard worked so hard to pull this off and what a success it was. All three of my sons, thank you. And of course my wonderful daughter-in-law Seana worked her little buns off to make this all a big success.

A very special thanks to Richard who loves to surprise me, he pulled this one off perfectly.

My lovely Sydney joined the party, Henry and Reilly missed it. Lacrosse games are more important than Oma's 80's birthday party. Richards kids were here also, so nice of them to make the trip from Brockport. Doug's Karen had put a "Memory Book" together, collecting photographs and letters from friends and relatives, Karen worked the floor.

Thank you all, it was the best!

Lovely summer and the beautiful memories of my birthday party linger on.

My son decided to sell his building on South Main Street, home of "Le Salon", his working achievement of the past 25 years. The closing date is set for end of July.

As a total surprise, my son was struck by a stroke on July 19th and was hospitalized for three days. It was a major shock to our family, especially me. Derek lost some memory, no physical damage. He and his dog Max stayed with me for several weeks. I took over the transfer of the Salon to the new owner, managed and sold furnishings from the salon and equipment on e-bay, cleaned and got the building ready for transfer of title. I was glad I was able to help.

I believe it was too much for Derek to handle, emotionally and physically, selling the building, giving up his business of 25 years. It was his life achievement. So sad and very stressful for me seeing my oldest son experience this set back, he seems too young for this. I have not accepted that my kids are getting older, they are still my kids.

Richard decided to move to "Ferris Hills" an independent senior citizen facility. He sold his house rather quickly and again I was the main coordinator for the second move within two weeks. I have to admit it was extremely stressful, physically and emotional.

My swimming exercise, the only outlet for myself, stopped abruptly with both these events almost happening the same time. I truly expected my life to glide along more smoothly in my 80's, however this was not the case. Derek's stroke really worried me more than I ever imagined. So totally unexpected. He appeared fairly healthy all these years, but was a smoker. I was told that a stroke happens very unexpectedly, out of the blue. His co-workers send him home to rest after he explained of a headache and not feeling well. It was eight hours before I found out and was able to get him to a hospital. After his hospital stay he recuperated at my house for several weeks, till he felt strong enough to be on his own and continue his work as a hairdresser.

Selling "Le Salon" and renting a chair in a hair salon on Main Street is cutting his work load and he is trying very hard to keep his very loyal customers happy. Many of his clients have been with him more than 20 years. He did quit smoking and is doing well.

Richard has settled in at Ferris Hill quite well, a very big adjustment for him. He is trying hard to fit into this new community. I am crossing my fingers and hope he will adjust. It was his idea after all.

He has a very spacious two bedroom apartment, full-sized kitchen and a lovely balcony. I thought, once he has all his "stuff" around him, the pictures and portraits of his children and grandchildren, he will feel more comfortable.

Fairly soon after Richard moved I realized he needed ME along with his stuff. He expects me to spend more time with him and wants me there for every meal. I am trying to put myself back together, but I feel it is all too much. I am on overload, something has to give. Also, Richard needs a knee replacement and has a difficult time walking, using a cane and sometimes a walker. He has fallen several times in his apartment, tripping and his knee gives out. He has been admitted to the hospital twice, once for a fall and one time for pseudo gout. Very painful and no cure.

Richard met with Dr. M. and scheduled knee replacement surgery for June, 2020 to be performed at Thompson Hospital.

Well, that date was too far off for Richard, he got impatient and he found Dr. G. They managed to set an earlier date for the surgery on March18th at Highland hospital. One week before the surgery we agreed Richard should move in with me, for the time being; it would be better to recuperate at my house after he completed re-habilitation at Clark Meadow. That was a good thought.

The Pandemic

Just when I thought life would settle to some degree of normalcy, the deadly Corona Virus or Covid 19 hit the world like a spit fire. The previous weeks we heard about a virus originating in China and it quickly traveled to Europe attacking healthy people in every country of the world, especially in Italy, Spain, France and Germany. We first were told it is a different and more severe strain of the flu. We respected that explanation but did not expect that this virus will affect the whole world and is highly contagious.

March 11, 2020 President Trump informed the Nation, the American people, via TV regarding the pandemic. We, the Nation found out at a later date that our President knew about the seriousness regarding the pandemic at a much earlier time, but did not inform the public early enough and/or take the virus serious enough to prevent this pandemic from spreading.

By March 16 schools were closed, public transportation, shops large and small, closed. Hair Parlors, fitness centers, restaurants, everything and all, except grocery stores and pharmacies remained open. President Trump kept reassuring the public that everything is under control, he down played the seriousness of this deadly Pandemic that had attacked our country and the world. The disease supposedly originated in the city of Wuhan, China, so President Trump calls the disease the Chinese virus.

All air traffic entering USA was stopped almost immediately. Before we understood what was going on, our whole country was quarantined. We watched TV all day long and half the night to stay informed. On March 16, a date that is always in my memory, the date my beloved Wuerzburg was bombed, we were told to quarantine in our homes. Two catastrophic events in my life time on the same date! 75 years apart!

We received notice that Richard's surgery date was canceled and all elective surgeries in all hospitals were put on hold. Hospital wards and beds were prepared for Corona virus patience. The death rate climbed rabidly and spread from State to State. It seems the elderly are mostly in danger. No vaccine available against the deadly Corona virus.

Since Richard was here at my house, he needed to stay and quarantine here. Ferris Hill went on immediate lock down. Nobody in, nobody out. We both appreciated very much that we were stuck here together. So many folks are by themselves, it is a lonely time for all. We were also lucky bringing some of Richards's clothes to my house from Ferris Hill, we snuck into his apartment later in the evening, so we would not meet up with any of the personnel or residents.

All restaurants were closed, only curbside pick-up and service.

Groceries can be ordered from the store to be delivered, however most of the time my 17 year old granddaughter Reilly is doing our grocery shopping. She brings it to my garage where it has to sit for several hours, before I can bring it in to the house. Then we are supposed to wipe down the milk cartons and food packages with sanitary wipes. Hoarders are cleaning out the grocery stores, with an immediate shortage of certain products like paper goods including toilet paper, paper towels and diapers. Disinfectant sanitary items are hardly available.

Covid cases are climbing every day with New York City taking the brunt of it. Soon hospitals were filled to capacity and the hospital staff is on overload. Traveling doctors and nurses from other states are brought to New York City to help out. They are called "Travel Nurses".

Thousands of people dying every day, NY City is running out of ventilators, hospital beds and caskets, bodies have to be stored in refrigerated trucks. Doctors, nurses and healthcare workers are at the verge of exhaustion. Everybody in our state is ordered to stay at home, wear masks and/or face shields. Keep social distance of six feet or more and no gatherings of four people at one time. Celebrations like High School Graduations, Weddings and Sporting Events were cancelled.

I pulled out my old Singer sewing machine, searched for left-over materials in a stowed away box, with the hope of making facemasks. That effort did not last long. The old Singer being in desperate need of an overhaul and was of no help at all.

People were furloughed from work or lost their jobs. Stay at home was the order for all. The pandemic is spreading like a wild fire and we don't have a vaccine. Working from home became the way for making a living for lots of folks.

President Donald Trump keeps re-assuring the nation this Covid virus will disappear once the warm weather rolls around. We, the people of this country believed his words and looked up to his leadership. Later on we found out how wrong he was.

Reilly graduated from High school that year and we could not attend her graduation. It was held at Bristol Mountain ski resort. The students rode the ski lift up to the top of the mountain where they were presented their diplomas. She will attend Binghamton University. So proud of you Rei, and love you so much.

My Grandchildren

Robinella

It has been an especially long and hard winter stretching to the middle of May. Everybody is longing to go out doors to catch the first warm sunrays and spring breezes.

Since we were all quarantined at home, we considered ourselves very fortunate if we own any size of greenspace and/or a small patio to enjoy the outdoors. I feel terribly bad for the folks who are stuck in apartments and cannot even get a breath of fresh air.

Grandson Henry's 21 birthday was celebrated on Easter Sunday without much fanfare. My family showed up in my garage, keeping the proper social distance and wearing their masks. They dropped off a delicious Easter dinner of Baked Ham, potato casserole, and salad, plus several desserts for Richard and me.

Poor Henry, not a Bar open in town. He finally could be a legal customer.

This was the only time we got to see my family in the next two months.

Mother's Day passed and so did my birthday, without celebration.

By May 15th some stores could open with many restrictions from our State Government. I took the opportunity to venture out with a mask covering my face and follow the required guide lines. First stop the outdoor Garden store. Bring some new life with flowers and plants to my patio.

I purchased some lettuce seedlings. This has been a very successful venture for me over the last years growing lettuce in my raised garden bed on the patio and herbs in flower pots. I get a lot of mileage out of my home-grown lettuce, eating at least three side salads per week. I am also very successful with tomatoes, all grown in a pot, and let's not forget basil, chives and parsley.

One of my favorite activities in spring time is working in my mini gardens which now consists of playing with my flower pots, moving them from one side of the deck across to the other. My deck is actually my front entrance to my home and I prefer to call it the "courtyard". It is fenced in. Mostly I transplant the smaller plants from the plain plastic containers to more decorative ceramic pots which are a little more colorful and attractive. I love colors!

A beautiful pink cascading geranium now hangs on one arm of an iron rod, the other side holds some lovely purplish and pink colored mixed posies which my neighbor dropped off in early spring for no reason at all. What a lovely gesture, I am sure it brightened his day, as it did mine. So thoughtful and it surely makes you think of spring in the middle of a snow storm. A pretty yellow flower pot hangs on the other side of the fence, I don't recognize the name. I bought that one for myself, simply because I liked it. Close by is another yellow smaller pot, some Begonias, a gift for Mother's Day and are very special to me, a gift from my granddaughter Sydney.

Every day I water my plants and keep a close eye on the growing progress and also deadhead the flowering plants. It is relaxing and brings me joy and I get away from the never ending terrible news on television.

Lots of chirping has been going on around here. All thru the winter I have been feeding yellow finches, hanging feed bags in my two small trees. These tiny birds entertain me every day, they congregate in my small garden area. I also have noticed several Robins flying in and out. Wish I would see a Cardinal, my favorite small bird, but no such luck.

I have never been a serious bird watcher, hardly know their names. I know some fly south in winter and return in spring. Some even hang around, like the little finches, and they provide lots of enjoyment, as long as I provide the food.

I have noticed one of the Robins flying into one particular flower pot which is filled with some lovely orange/red colored Mums. A very busy Robin selected this particular plant to build her nest in, collecting grasses and anything else she can use as construction material. By the next day this architectural wonder is almost complete in the midst of my Mum plant. A second Robins is not helping very much with the work efforts, he is more like a guard, keeping an eye on the progress and the safety of the nest.

I notice the first Robin was a little larger in size than the guard, so I figure number one is the female.

I named her Robinella.

I talked to her daily whenever I am on the patio, hoping she might as well get used to my presence and my voice, after all I live here and we have to share the court yard.

Maybe a day or two after the completion of the nest I spotted a beautiful little turquois colored egg. I was delighted, what a miracle. Three more tiny eggs followed, one each day.

Robinella was a busy expectant mom and soon started to sit on her eggs. The male Robin was always close by either sitting on the fence and/or making sure I was doing no harm.

My problem was, how do I water my Mums? I had a very old, small watering can with a very long spout and I watered around the rim of the flower pot, trying not to get the nest wet which was located in the center. I did not want to see the nest float away. It was built very solid, like glued together and stuck to the soil.

Robinella was sitting on her eggs almost three weeks before lots of activity started. She was in and out of the nest about every 20 minutes while father Robin sat on the fence and watched. Soon a small crack appeared on one of the eggs and a little naked piece of skin with scrawny legs appeared. It was rather ugly, reminded me of a piece of uncooked chicken. I kept peeking into the nest once or twice a day trying to keep my distance giving Robinella the privacy and time she required to do her busy and important work.

During the night the parents picked up every little piece of egg shell from the nest and carried it away. I learned later that Robins carry the egg shells away from the nest and deposit them somewhere else, so predators get distracted from the location of the nest. How clever!

Every day for the next days a new little bird appears in the nest. One each day until there are four. Fuzzy hair appeared on their skin almost immediately and they looked more appealing each day. Robinella and the daddy were busy feeding worms to their tiny offspring's, the very tiny creatures with a big mouth. It was a miracle to watch how these ugly, naked things developed into beautiful little birds with nutrients only from worms.

Their little mouth was always wide open to receive more worms and several times I was tempted to stick my little finger into their mouths.

The Mums did very well with little water, they are in full bloom and hiding the birdies quite well. In about two weeks' time the birdies had grown enough to attempt to fly.

I had a doctor's appointment in the morning and returned home about noon. I went to check on my little brood. All but one were gone. Apparently the little runt was not brave enough to join the group.

It kept on peeping, "Mama where are you, come and get me". From inside of the dining room I tried to keep an eye on the patio and watch out for momma, but she did not come along. The poor little thing kept on chirping, it was not a happy sound, more like a panicky sound. I thought maybe I should help the birdie along trying to shoo it out of the nest. It spread his wings, flew up maybe half a foot, but something held it back. It was something similar to a bungee cord. Quick action was required and I grabbed the bird. A very thin long string was wrapped around one little leg and the birdie was permanently attached to the nest. Apparently when Robinella built the nest she used string as part of the construction material. Very carefully I unwrapped that horrible string (or whatever it was) which by that time was all the way up the little creature's leg. I carefully freed the bird and placed it on a nearby fence post. It flew to a patio chair, than dropped to the ground.

Oh, I so wished the mother would show up and tell its offspring what to do.

In the meantime the window cleaners showed up, (annual spring cleaning) and with big concerns and instructions I told them to watch out for a little bird, it is hopping around somewhere. The window cleaners helped looking, but no birdie insight. We could not spot it anywhere. I was hoping it went into a bush for cover and safety. A little while later Robinella showed up, a big worm hanging from her peak looking for the little one. I am so glad she showed up rather than abandon her baby, but the little bird could not be found. She soon flew away. Unfortunately the little birdie had disappeared.

I went on with the rest of my day. Later that afternoon I stepped into my garage. I heard a peep. Here was the little bird sitting on the arm of a lawn chair waiting for me. One more last good bye, I am sure it recognized me. I shooed it out of the garage into a nearby bush. Good bye baby Robinella, hope to see you next year.

The Pandemic Goes On

By now, the Covid Pandemic has taken over the world with no relief in sight.

The virus is not under control and the southern States are being hit hard. The political atmosphere is getting to the point where the nation is totally divided between Republicans and Democrats. Organized rioters demonstrate in most major cities each and every night. The "Black Live's Matter" movement is in high gear, high profile murder cases disrupt the country and add more confusion to the already explosive atmosphere. Police Departments all over the country are under attack and are being scrutinized.

By the end of June, Richard is able to visit his apartment at Ferris Hills with many restrictions imposed on all their residents and guests. Dining rooms are still closed and meals have to be served in the residents apartments. Residents are not allowed to dine together. No meetings, entertainment, or get-togethers, too many restrictions. Everybody needs to wear a face mask and stay in their apartment. We are all prisoners in our own home.

Loneliness effects the young and the old. It is especially difficult for the residents of nursing facilities who cannot receive visitors, not even family. They die alone. School children are not allowed to visit their friends. The suicide rate in younger people is escalating.

Richard and I read a lot. I cook for the two of us and keep myself busy as best as I can. As long as I am able to go outside I am all right. With age comes experience and wisdom and let's not forget patience. Older adults have higher levels of empathy and compassion. Besides that, we consider ourselves lucky, we have each other and we are able to sit on our patio and go for a short walk. It makes such a difference and I feel blessed. I lived thru difficult times before and I survived and I will do my best to survive this pandemic.

Middle of July we celebrated Richard's 86th birthday with his kids arriving from out of State. It's a little different this year, we all have to keep our distance. His family rented a house on the lake and had to be quarantined for the entire week. We visited every day, but it was on a low key visitation schedule. Groceries where ordered from Wegmans and all meals where prepared on premises. We visited mostly outside on the patio, by the lake, not inside the house.

By all means, it still was a wonderful week having Richard's family here from Virginia and Brockport and all had a great time. We practiced social distance of six feet and wore the required masks. We managed and enjoyed the special time we could celebrate together.

By the end of summer, restaurants were allowed to reopen at 25% capacity and so could hair salons. However it makes it very difficult for these business to survive and the unemployment rate is at a very high level.

By end of August Reilly left for her first year of college to Binghamton University. Henry left the following week for SUNY Potsdam. Covid testing is necessary for all students before they can enter college.

Derek moved to an apartment in Canandaigua. It will be much better for him to be close to his family here in town, being within walking distance to his place of work on Main Street. Again it was a difficult move, relocating from a ground floor apartment to an upstairs flat. He thinks positive and he is looking forward to all the conveniences Canandaigua city living has to offer.

Sydney and boyfriend Ryan purchased their first home in Rochester. We have not seen it yet. It sounds like it is a big improvement from their last flat which we never got to see. I was told it was very small but cost effective and it allowed them to save up the necessary dollars needed for a down payment for a larger residence. The new house is closer to Strong Memorial Hospital where Sydney works at the "Golisano's Children's Hospital". There also is a small yard for their young black Lab, Gracie, who needed a bit more space to stretch her long legs. She is a lively young pup with lots of energy.

President Trump still did not take this pandemic seriously, he downplayed the virus and refuses to wear a mask. The political atmosphere is at an all-time high, Democrats and Republicans are fighting to win the presidential election in November. Rioting is happening in many cities, large or small, mostly about "Black Lives Matter" and the uprising against the Police Departments is escalating. This country is in a mess, worst I have ever seen. Worse than in the 60's.

October 2nd 2020 President Trump is admitted at Walter Reed Medical Center for the treatment of Corona virus.

My granddaughter Reilly who is studying bio-chemistry at University of Binghamton is sent home from school (after only a few weeks being there) she herself testing negative for the virus. Some classmates had tested positive. Four days later at home, she tests positive. Her symptoms are fever and cough plus total exhaustion. She sleeps most of the time. Both parents, along with Reilly, are quarantined and soon Stuart turned positive. Seana remains negative but needs to remain quarantined. They are under strict watch by the County who checks on them daily, making sure nobody leaves the house. Actually somebody drives by the house, looking for activity and calls them on the phone.

Henry's college students in Potsdam are holding up well, the students have to test for the virus twice a week. So far they kept the virus off campus.

This summer, Richard was admitted twice to Strong Hospital with complications of the pancreas. I dropped him off at the entrance of the hospital, and immediately the staff whisked him away in a wheelchair. The only communication with him is done by phone, the doctors also call me. I either drive around for hours waiting for him to be released or drive home, than back to Strong Hospital to pick him up. It is a long and exhausting wait.

He did not feel well and was losing weight. I moved him back into my home again, it is easier than running back and forth to Ferris Hill.

In late September we took a Sunday afternoon drive and stop at an "Open House" in the "Villas", the development where I live, where he used to own his last house. He liked the house, puts an offer in and within two hours his offer was accepted. Two weeks later the deal was closed. He decided he did not want to live at Ferris Hill any longer, too many restrictions. Now he has till the end of October to move all his belongings from Ferris Hill to his new pad. I agree, it is a very lovely home, two bedrooms, two baths, lovely patio plus two car garage. A good move!

He is familiar with the neighborhood, the same location as his last house. He acclimated very quickly. Being closer to me makes life a lot easier for both of us and I have to admit it is definitely much more convenient having him close by. He hated the walk thru the lobby at Ferris Hill, to the elevator and down the long hall to his quarters. It will be so much easier for him to step from his back door into his garage into the car. Now the packing will start all over again.

We have "Help" lined up for all the packing of his belongings. It is a lot of work (since he did not get rid of any of his worldly possessions with the last move) coordinating all the necessary preparations to get ready for a move. New carpets were ordered to be installed, tearing out the perfectly good vinyl floors. We hired an aide, nice girl who will come to help out when Richard does not feel up to speed, the cleaning lady Terri will take care of the rest. Between the two ladies, the house is always clean and the laundry is done. We always have dinner together, me doing the cooking or we order our meals in, since most restaurants are still closed.

Richard, myself, and our families are holding up reasonably well under the current living restrictions, getting used to being house bound. I try to take a daily walk around the block to keep myself mobile, wave at a neighbor or stop for a brief chat, all from a distance.

President Trump lost the election last year and the new democratic President, Joe Biden was sworn in last January. The Pandemic carries on. It has been more than a year. By the end of February 2021 we have lost 500,000 people in the USA to the Covid virus. These are more victims than we have lost in World War 1 and 2 together. People are still in quarantine, restrictions have become somewhat relaxed in the summer of 2021. Anybody flying into NY State or traveling by car has to quarantine for two weeks. Masks are a must anywhere you go and social distancing is required and necessary.

We finally have vaccinations approved against Covid 19 but it appears to be very difficult for the organizers to make the necessary arrangements to vaccinate every person in the USA. Some folks have to travel to the next county, even Syracuse or Buffalo to receive their shot in the arm. Just another total confusion created by our Government. Most people, especially the older generation from 65 years of age and up, are so anxious to receive their vaccination, they stand in line for hours.

The first vaccine was produced by Pfizer Pharmaceuticals, along came Moderna vaccination and a third one manufactured by Johnson and Johnson.

Richard and I received our 1st shot in the arm on January 21st, the second one on February 21st. We got Moderna and consider ourselves very lucky being in the first group of eligible folks in the age group of 65 and older. We were also lucky to only have to drive to Thompson Hospital for the injection. A third shot, called a Booster was administered to us six months after the second shot, so we consider ourselves well protected.

Richard was recently diagnosed with Follicular Lymphoma. He received his first Chemo treatment the end of February 2021. The infusion took six hours and I must say he tolerated the treatment very well, just feeling tired and exhausted. The following Friday will be the second injection. I am pleasantly surprised how well he is holding up after the Chemo treatments.

Summer of 2021 my beautiful Granddaughter Sydney finished her Master's degree in teaching nursing. She is employed at "Golisano's Children's Hospital" at Strong Memorial and loves her work. She also started teaching nursing (one day a week) at St. John's Fisher College. Now she is an adjunct Professor. Her life is moving in a well-planned direction, I am so proud of her. She and Ryan also became engaged.

Her wedding to Ryan is set for July 31, 2022. We hope some Covid restrictions (like wearing a mask in public) will be lifted by summer and life will be somewhat closer to normal, meaning before Covid. I am looking forward to this event, it will be a wonderful celebration. Karen and Doug will also be able to travel here, have not seen them in a while.

A second wedding will take place in September in Charlottesville, VA. Richards' grandson JT will be married to a lady named Chesa, she is a native of Japan. Also looking forward to that event. We definitely need some fancy new clothes for both these special events.

Henry graduate from Potsdam this spring, Reilly is studying hard. By now, all my family had Covid at least once, some even twice. The young folks deal much better with it than us old folks.

Last spring, Richard relinquished his automobile. I do all the driving. Since he always needs to have a little excitement and fun, he purchased a golf cart to whip around in our "Villa" complex. This all- terrain vehicle gives him the freedom he desires to be mobile. He got a plastic enclosure for it, so he can use it in the rain and most of the winter. It also has really big tires and moves fairly well in the snow, however he did get stuck in a snow bank once. It was an easy push-out.

Full Circle

ANOTHER WAR

Fast forward now to February 2022. We are experiencing a tough winter. It came in like a lamb, with a "no snow" Thanksgiving or Christmas of 2021 but we are making up for it now. My daily walks are almost non-existing, so Richard and I go for an afternoon ride, purchasing a few groceries, stop for a takeout from Starbucks coffee (I think I am addicted to it, but who cares) and drive to the lake to watch the ducks, geese and other birds. The enjoyments of our "Golden Years", at least we are enjoying it together. Rarely do we go to a restaurant in fear of Covid, even so Richard received a 4th vaccine, a trial vaccination for folks with underlying health conditions.

Another War!

In the middle of February 2022 Russia invaded Ukraine. I did not think this would happen, also Russia has been trying for about 14 years to invade this country. This time I get to watch it on TV, I am not there. I feel for the people as they are evacuating their homes, walking away from all their worldly possession and crossing the borders into Poland, Romania and Germany. These border countries are so gracious, opening their homes to take in the refugees. I see mothers holding their children's hand plus a small suitcase, some push a stroller or baby carriage and even carrying a small pet. They are fleeing and leaving their beautiful apartments with all their belongings behind.

I am glued to the television and it almost feels like I am experiencing war time for a second time.

I see myself right there, this is me, that small child with the pink hat hanging on to her mother's hand and staring at her mother's navy blue shoes. They walk like I walked, no final destination, evacuating into an unknown future. They leave it all behind and they hope husbands and fathers will return unharmed from the battle. I have to admit this is affecting me more than I ever thought it would.

Do you realize what mental harm a war can do to little children? They will never go home again to the place they called home, they will never sleep in the same bed again or play with the same toys.

Read this last paragraph over, please.

These children are on the way to NO place, their life is forever changed and it will never ever be the same. They don't know this yet, they don't know what the future has in store for them. I know, I have been there. They are trying to be brave and hold on to their mother's hand so they won't get lost riding on the buses or trains or walking with the masses. Behind them their houses are shelled and the dust covers it all.

I am watching this happening on TV right now and I am totally affected. I don't sleep well, my thoughts are back to when I was a child. I talk to my relatives in Germany, they tell me what they see and hear. They are totally appalled. Remember "NEVER AGAIN". The German Nations promise to their countrymen. NEVER AGAIN will we get involved in another war. We have to stay out of the conflict between Ukraine and Russia. I pray, Germany does not have to get involved.

The Ukrainians are fleeing their country, many go as far as to

Germany. The children have to enter the German school system, they don't speak the German language. Ukrainians are wandering to any European country that will take them in. Housing is in short supply for the influx of people.

"The Russians are coming, the Russians are coming" just like I heard in 1945. People are fleeing from the Russians sent by President Putin, who has a strong resemblance to Stalin and Hitler.

I watch the bombings of the buildings, people's homes, hospitals and schools. The beautiful buildings that were re-built after World War 2 are being shelled and leveled again. I feel the pain, I guess I never forgot. I feel especially and extremely sorry for the older people, they are experiencing all of this for the second time. Many of them will not leave their property or country. They are waiting for "whatever happens".

There will always be war in the world. I pray it will not affect me directly, we might have to send our Military to fight for us. That is bad enough.

But to live thru a war and the after years is horrific. I am hoping nobody has to experience it.

Summer 2022

Just to mention, by now about 900,000 Americans have lost their lives from Covid.

Richard and I both had contracted the disease in April 2022, we were ok. Very tired, cough and the symptoms are very similar to the flu. Richard's symptoms are a bit more severe, I recovered after four days.

A news reporter is telling us that the number of Covid deaths in these United States has reached the milestone of one million people.

More and more people are contracting the disease. Being immunized helps most folks not to be admitted to hospital, but you still can catch it and obviously more than once. Unfortunately, there are still many people that refuse to get vaccinated.

Richard's housekeeper is coming to help out almost every day. She prepares breakfast and lunch most days and it gives me a break from constantly worrying "is he all right"? I definitely can feel I am getting older and don't want to push my luck.

It already has been a busy spring and it will continue throughout the summer.

Henry graduated from SUNY Potsdam and Richard's granddaughter Kelly from Cornell University.

A wonderful Bridal shower was held for Sydney at the Canandaigua Country Club in June and now we are looking forward to her wedding, July 31, 2022.

Sydney's and Ryan's wedding took place at the before mentioned date, exactly 26 years after my husband's death. It was a beautiful day for all our family and many friends. We will not forget the wonderful celebration.

What a party it was.

A new generation will start their journey.

I like to thank you all for hanging in there with me, putting up with me and my story. I did the best I could and hope you will do the same during your life time.

Love you all

Sydney's wedding 2022

*One last look back
... Afterword*

It is time to reflect a bit, sit back and smell the roses, time to slow down.

I enjoy spending more quiet time by myself, occasionally a dinner out with friends or family. I lost interest in traveling, cooking and entertaining. Time for someone else to do these "chores", time for the next generation to take over.

Altogether, I feel I had a comfortable life. I was successful in my career as a Real Estate Broker, even so it was stressful at times but also very rewarding, helping people find their dream home.

My parents where loving and kind and both loved me very much. They raised me the best they could under difficult circumstances. - I survived.

I lived thru World War 2 - I survived.

I immigrated to another country, leaving my parents and relatives behind to start life in another world – I survived

I raised, along with their loving father, three very caring and great sons to be successful human beings, not an easy chore - I survived.

I am spoiling three beautiful grandchildren, I am proud to be their loving "Oma".

I had the good fortune to love two wonderful men, - both loved me to the moon and back.

I hope I did not do any harm to this earth or any living creature. I always realized that we do live on a beautiful planet, so please take care of it. Don't take it for granted.

I did not win a Nobel Prize or other significant awards, but I hope I contributed a bit to the wellbeing of others, brought happiness to my family and friends, and wish that they can experience peace, love, satisfaction and happiness to the fullest during their life time.

I hope all your life's will be blessed with happiness and success and you will remember where you come from.

I hope you will remember me as a strong, honest, loving and kind Mom and Oma, who did her best.

I wish for all to remember me well and understand my way of "reasoning" thru out my lifetime.

When I am gone, remember me with kindness and love. I am doing my best!

Acknowledgements

Many, many thanks and lots of gratitude go to my neighbor and friend, Author John Robert Allen, who encouraged me to write my "story".

I never wrote more than a school essay and letters, many, many letters in the German language of course.

With John's constant encouragement and guidance, I completed writing "my memoirs" in about three years. It took commitment and discipline to myself and I am proud I completed this project. Hip hip hurray for me.

Thank you John for helping me open my small world.

A big "thank you" goes to another neighbor and Author, Gerald Marsh. "Jed" helped along with spelling correction and encouragement. He kept telling me "when I read your story, I feel like I am there and you are talking to me". That was what I was trying to accomplish.

I also like to mention our writing group here in the "Canandaigua Villas". Without this group I never would have started to write. I joined this encouraging group more for fun than writing, but we kept pushing each other forward and after three years I finished my project.

Thank you ladies and gentlemen for your encouragement!

Last but not least, a big thank you to Richard for his patience, encouragement and continues love. He put up with all my frustrations and impatience during the last three years.

Thank you to all these wonderful people for being my support when I needed you.

Love you all and God bless!

An ordinary life, never boring

Made in the USA
Las Vegas, NV
12 March 2023

68967607R00135